# A PRACTICAL HANDBOOK
# FOR THE
# BOYFRIEND

### For Every Guy Who Wants to Be One
### FOR EVERY GIRL WHO WANTS TO BUILD ONE!

# FELICITY HUFFMAN
# & PATRICIA WOLFF

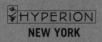

HYPERION
NEW YORK

Library of Congress Cataloging-in-Publication Data

Huffman, Felicity.
    A practical handbook for the boyfriend : for every guy who wants to be one, for every girl who wants to build one / Felicity Huffman & Patricia Wolff. — 1st ed.
        p.   cm.
    ISBN: 1-4013-0291-2
    ISBN-13: 978-1-4013-0291-7
    1. Man-woman relationships. 2. Dating (Social customs) 3. Single men—Life skills guides. I. Wolff, Patricia. II. Title.

HQ801.H92 2007
646.7'7—dc22

                                              2006046823

Hyperion books are available for special promotions and premiums. For details contact Michael Rentas, Assistant Director, Inventory Operations, Hyperion, 77 West 66th Street, 12th floor, New York, New York 10023, or call 212-456-0133.

Art direction by Michelle Ishay
Book design by Kris Tobiassen

FIRST EDITION

10 9 8 7 6 5 4 3 2 1

*This book is dedicated to Bill Macy, the best boyfriend and husband a girl could have.*

*—FH*

*This book is dedicated to my grandmother Henri Kushkin, who at the age of 96 tells great stories about her boyfriends, especially Charlie Hoffman, her first boyfriend from third grade.*

*—PW*

# CONTENTS

# ACKNOWLEDGMENTS

*We would like to thank all good and bad BFs who made our* lives miserable and happy, and all the GFs who over the years have stayed up with us swapping love and war stories, laughing, crying, raging, and talking dirty, while perched on kitchen and bathroom counters all across the globe.

Thanks to Bob Miller of Hyperion, Richard Abate of ICM, and Michael Ritchie: We're sure you were great BFs before you hung up your spurs, and now are great presidents, agents, and understanding bosses.

To Brenda Copeland: GF, editor, and stone-cold cool chick. And to Michelle Ishay for her great research skills and all-around good taste.

To the first GFs we knew, our mothers: Thank you for the guidance and the patience.

To the first BFs we knew, our fathers: Thanks for showing us what great BF material looks like.

To our sisters and brothers who guided us, championed us, and taught us to tell the difference between the good, the bad, and the ugly.

To Bill Macy for your suggestion to cut down on our use of the word blow job (on the page, anyway).

To the Atlantic Theater Company, for twenty years of skinny-dipping with BFs and potential BFs.

And finally to Clark Gregg, an honorary GF if ever there was one.

### *P.S. A note to our readers:*

Although we have tried to hit the key aspects of the complicated, ever changing world of the Boyfriend, we are sure there are details, subjects, and points of view we have omitted or just plain didn't think of. Feel free to write us c/o Hyperion at 77 West 66th Street, New York, NY 10023, to tell us what we missed or got wrong, or just to share a good boyfriend or girlfriend story. You are also welcome to use the complaint box as you exit.

# A PRACTICAL
# HANDBOOK
## FOR THE
# BOYFRIEND

# INTRODUCTION

**We take pleasure in presenting to you, the men of America,** this first edition of *A Practical Handbook for the Boyfriend*. Whether you're a good guy or a bad boy, single or attached, you will find this an indispensable guide to your girlfriend or girlfriend-to-be. You'll also find it an essential collection of ideas, information, and assorted survival skills that will surely come in handy.

Think of this as your AAA guide to love, a decoder ring, a relationship road map, and your very own GPS—Girlfriend Positioning System. We'll steer you toward the right turns and help you avoid the wrong ones so that you don't ever have to change a flat in A Town Called Lame, population one. In addition to offering interesting recipes for the holidays (okay, not really), this book will give tasty tips on the following:

- How to apologize without really apologizing

- How to look like you're listening while you're thinking about other things (keep eye contact at all times, but if busted, repeat the phrase "You're so pretty, I'm distracted")

- How to tell if her "no" means "yes," or her "yes" means "no"

- How to avoid long phone conversations

- How to survive her driving

- How to buy the last-minute present

- How to charm the pants off of her (literally)

- How to avoid talking about your "feelings"

- How to pretend you have "feelings"

- How to pretend you're deep

- How to talk dirty (a beginner's guide)

- How to convince her farting in bed is a sign of your commitment

- How to have sex without intimacy (Oops, forgot who we were talking to. Never mind.)

***You may think that you're the first guy to try to understand*** women and come up empty-handed, but you're not. Men have been scratching their heads about the fairer sex since the beginning of time.

Think of the first boyfriend, Adam. You think he wasn't baffled by his girlfriend? You bet he was. Now, there's a guy who could have used this book. You may not think he needed it—after all, he was alone in paradise, had some snacks, and Eve was already naked. But we beg to differ.

Their problems weren't over money, getting out of dinner with her parents, or his addiction to online poker. No, their issues revolved around a small piece of red fruit. God said, "Don't eat it." Eve said, "If you love me you'll bite." The poor guy had God on one side and Eve on the other; talk about a rock and a hard place. Adam tried to reason with his girl, warning her of the dangers of breaking the one rule God had made, but she wouldn't listen. From her point of view it wasn't about the apple or God (she wasn't hungry and had never even met the Big Guy in the sky), it was about whether her boyfriend took her seriously and understood her feelings. Sound familiar? In her mind, Adam was trying to control her . . . again. Talk about a power trip. Who died and left him in charge? There he was telling her what to eat, what not to eat, and by the way, was this "don't eat the apple" thing his way of letting her know he thought she was fat? Great.

But maybe Adam was just a regular guy, trying to toe the line with The Man and trying to keep his girlfriend happy. It couldn't have been easy. We girlfriends can be a lot to handle. We demand intimacy. We ask a lot of questions: "What are you thinking about?" "Do you love me?" "How come we never talk?" And the transitions are murder. One minute we're lying around happy and naked (think Eve), and the next minute we're dressed to kill, goose-stepping all over your heart (think Eva Braun).

Or maybe what happened that day was just a moment of profound miscommunication:

"I thought you said take a bite!"

"No, I said let's not fight!"

And afterward they found themselves thrown out of paradise and faced with having to find a new place to live (and in terms of stress levels, moving is second only to death in how it can affect a couple).

Biblical scholars have offered various interpretations of the story of Adam and Eve, but we'll never know what really happened. Still we are certain of one thing: Men and women will never see, hear, or feel things in just the same way. That was as true in the Garden of Eden as it is in the Garden State of New Jersey or anywhere else on God's Green Earth.

So what's a guy to do? Unfortunately, there is no perfect answer. We can't teach you what to expect from your GF because she will never be the same from one day to the next, or even from one moment to the next. Being with a woman can be like living in a time machine where you are zapped every few hours into another female mood without warning. We can't change that, but we can help demystify some of your girlfriend's behavior so that when the woman you love transports you once again to a galaxy far, far away, you'll have the skills you need to quickly orient yourself and deftly master the situation. Our job is to make sure you are prepared.

\*   \*   \*

**Now, you may not be interested in being a boyfriend, and** that's fine. But there may come a day when you want to be thought of as Mr. Right, and not Mr. Right Now. When you do, you'll want this book in your back pocket, right next to your wallet and that ribbed-for-pleasure condom. Read it from cover to cover or jump to the chapter you need. Become an expert in a couple of hours. Or just look like one.

# CHAPTER 1

# ALL WOMEN ARE CRAZY

***Okay, okay, okay, we've heard it before, the two clichés*** that divide the gender camps: All women are crazy. All men are jerks.

We know you're not jerks (well, some guys are, but not you, you're reading this book) and believe it or not, all women are not crazy. So why does so much of what women do seem to baffle you? Because REALITY IS RELATIVE. Still confused? Don't worry, we're just getting started.

First, let's review a little biology. Mice and humans share 95 percent of the same DNA, so while we are largely the same, that 5 percent accounts for some major differences: fur, tail, and a penchant for eating one's young, for starters. As for the differences between the sexes, women have more neurons connecting the right and left sides of their brain than men do—four times as many, in fact.

But whatever . . . we're not here to gloat. The most discernible variation between the biology of men and women lies in that tiny little X chromosome/Y chromosome thing, which, as it turns out, is not such a tiny little thing at all. Study after study reveals substantial differences in perceptions, attitudes, priorities, communication styles, handwriting, hairstyles, and furniture selection. Most women are concerned with relationships, people, diet, clothing, and physical appearance. Most men are concerned with sex, sports, work, money, cars, news, politics, and the mechanics of things. Sure, we're generalizing here, but you get the point. Basically, we're different in every way. We might as well be mice and men.

## *Girl Math*

So we see things differently, but that's not all; we feel things differently, too. Women are in touch with a much wider range of feelings than men, and those feelings are much more intense. A man's emotional checklist is pretty basic:

☐ Am I hungry?

☐ Am I sleepy?

☐ Am I horny?

If he's content in all three areas, he's pretty much okay. A woman's emotional checklist reads more like a Russian novel. It's long, complicated, and confusing, and you spend a lot of time trying to keep the characters straight.

Because we see and feel things differently, it follows that we also are different in the way we make decisions. You guys want a repeatable, defined decision-making process, and you always will. Something like this:

A. It's dinnertime.

B. I want ribs, plus they'll have the TV on at the restaurant, so I can watch the game.

C. Let's go to Bruno's.

The equation looks like this: A + B = C
Makes sense, right?
For your girlfriend, the process is something like this:

A. It's dinnertime.

B. I wonder if we go out too much—or maybe not enough—have I paid my Visa bill? Bruno's has that wall paneling that reminds me of that party I went to years ago—THAT was awful—everyone made fun of my hair. Do I have to wash my hair if we go out?—why do boys always want to eat so late?—ribs are really yummy but then I'll be stuffed from dinner, and late-night sex won't be as fun—everything is just too much!

C. No, I can't go to dinner, and I feel overwhelmed, why can't you understand?

Her equation looks like this:
$$A + B \times L(!!) \div K \sqrt{S} \geq T ** + S(R) = C$$

We call it Girl Math.

Your GF will feel that she has been working in a linear and careful manner, that her decision is both logical and defensible. You'll watch this process in stunned silence and think, "She's crazy."

You guys work hard to try to unravel the mysteries of women. You give it your best effort. We know that. The confusion doesn't come from lack of trying or lack of practice. But that's not what works with women. Familiarity does not breed understanding.

We know a man who has seven sisters, and we know fathers with many daughters. And then there are polygamists, or Jude Law, for that matter. You would assume they are the go-to guys for all things female. Wrong. The father with the daughters, the brother with the sisters, the guy with six wives are all equally in the dark when it comes to the riddle of women. And by the way, we've never met Jude Law, but according to the tabloid trail, he's as clueless as everyone else with a penis.

# *Keep Crazy in the Bottle*

We're aware you think we're crazy. We don't agree (we make perfect sense to ourselves), but we don't want you to run screaming for the hills, so we like to "keep crazy in the bottle" for at least the first four or five months, until we've got you hooked. Then we let it seep out little by little. The real us. The real way we think and feel. We can't bottle it up forever.

## *Girl Crazy*

Remember the movie *White Men Can't Jump?* Rosie Perez is in bed with her BF, Woody Harrelson, when she turns to him (we're paraphrasing here) and says, "Honey, I need a glass of water." So he stumbles out of bed and brings back the water. "NO!" she screams. "I don't want the water. I want you to understand that I am thirsty, and be with me in the *feeling* of wanting water! I didn't need the water, you asshole! I needed you to hear me and be there for me, in my feelings."

When we're upset, men understandably try to change our mood by offering solutions to our problems. We interpret this as discounting our feelings, which results in: "Why are you offering solutions when what I really want is empathy, and don't look at me like you think I'm crazy."

Does any of this sound familiar?

- Out of the blue, she'll burst into tears. When she's happy. When she's sad. Because you love her. Because you don't love her enough. Because you didn't call her back within the hour. Because it's Tuesday.

- All of a sudden she'll be pissed at you. When she's happy. When she's sad. Because you love her. Because you don't love her enough. Because you didn't call her back within the hour. Because it's Tuesday.

- She will expect you to read her mind, and when you don't, she will cry (because she is sad), and when you do, she will cry (because she is happy).

- She will say you don't spend enough time with her, and then, when you clear your day, she'll be busy.

- She will never put the tops on things, and then she'll freak out when stuff spills, and then she will get angry (as if the universe has turned on her), and then she will cry.

- She will put rice on the stove, make a phone call, and then be shocked when the rice burns. She will be mad at you for pointing out the obvious.

- She will say you don't buy her enough presents, and then she'll return the ones you do get her.

- She will say, "We never talk," and the minute you get in the car together, she will get on her cell phone.

That all seems pretty crazy, right? Not to her. "Crazy" suggests that there is no rhyme or reason to what women do or how they feel. But there *is* rhyme, and there *is* reason. It's just different from yours. It's like having a pet. You keep looking at your cat and thinking, "She won't bark, she won't fetch, and she keeps coughing up fur balls." Reality check: It's a cat. You can't expect her to do dog things. If you do, she's going to look crazy. In the same way, if you apply "guy logic" to "girl behavior," what you come up with is "crazy" (defined as: mentally deranged, demented, senseless, totally unsound). We'll say it again. It's not that women are crazy, it's that reality is relative.

## *Reality Is Relative*
## *What You See/What She Sees*

### *The Party*

*YOU SEE:* A rockin' good time. Pot in the upstairs bedroom. Two hot girls dancing by the pool.

*SHE SEES:* A disgusting, overaged kegger. Stoners you went to high school with. Two girls with vomit in their hair.

### *The Apartment*

*YOU SEE:* Your apartment that you just spent forever cleaning. Your cool black leather single-guy chair.

*SHE SEES:* Dust balls the size of a small terrier and Cheerios stuck on the side of the toaster. The grossest black leather chair ever (that is the first thing she's going to get rid of).

### *The Hardware Store*

*YOU SEE:* A club you belong to. Aisle after aisle of cool shit you need. Visions of your cool self in a muscle T, wrench in hand, fixing the kitchen sink, while your girlfriend watches you adoringly, to be followed by great sex on the linoleum.

*SHE SEES:* The one store she doesn't want to shop in. Aisle after aisle of boring, identical, incomprehensible shit. An afternoon spent waiting while you break her kitchen sink.

### The Car Next to You

**YOU SEE:** A very cool guy in a '57 Chevy with what looks to be a 308 with a four-barrel, and a hot chick.

**SHE SEES:** A fifty-year-old guy with a comb-over and a girl half his age.

## In a Nutshell

We're aware of the confusion and fear we strike in your hearts, and we hate it. So the extra effort you make to understand us is that much more appreciated. Men and women are so different: mentally, physically, sociologically; our likes, our dislikes. This wouldn't be a problem if we all lived in separate countries. We could visit each other every now and then, talk, have sex, even spend the whole week, then we would go back to Girl Land and you could return to Guyville. Our differences would be charming oddities instead of pull-your-hair-out aggravations. But we would miss you and would probably sneak over to your peninsula, following you around, asking how you were feeling. But that's not how it is.

We realize the knowledge that reality is relative won't change the war cry from "All women are crazy" to "I get it—we're just the same, except different!" No, your GF will continue to seem crazy to you; so will your mother and your sister and your second cousin twice removed (the one you made out with when you were twelve). But at least now you know why. You can stop looking for the GF who makes sense to you. She doesn't exist.

# *Top Ten Phrases to Translate (Okay, really twelve)*

......................................

**PRACTICAL CHEAT SHEET FOR THE BOYFRIEND (OR, WHAT THE HECK DOES SHE MEAN?)**

| *SHE SAYS:* | *SHE MEANS:* |
| --- | --- |
| *"You're working too hard!"* | *"You're not spending enough time with me."* |
| *"I don't want presents for my birthday."* | *"Get me something anyway— surprise me!"* |
| *"What are you thinking about?"* | *"Do you still love me?"* |
| *"Do you find Carol attractive?"* | *"But I'm prettier, right?"* |
| *"Are you in therapy?"* | *"I really like you—God, I hope you have your shit together." (This is a compliment.)* |
| *"How are the eggs?"* | *"Don't you think I'm the best girl who ever made you anything in your whole life?"* |
| *"No honey, I'm fine."* | *"You've really made me sad/angry/upset, and let's have a really long talk about it."* |
| *"Well, I think I'd better go."* | *"Beg me to stay."* |
| *"What do your friends think about us?"* | *"Are you falling in love with me?"* |
| *"Do you want to talk about it?"* | *"I wanna talk about it."* |
| *"Are you too tired to stay over?"* | *"I want you to stay over."* |
| *"Fuck you, I can't stand you."* | *"Fuck you, I can't stand you."* |

# CHAPTER 2

# BOY

## MEETS

## GIRL

# First Question: Do you want to be a boyfriend or a player?

It's a tough call. As a player, you have your freedom. As a player, you get to keep it light and avoid the part where she starts to expect things from you. You can avoid anniversaries, relationship discussions, and dinner with her parents. As a player, you can jump from girl to girl and not owe anybody anything. You can get in, get out, and not get yelled at, which clearly has its advantages and is a lot of fun. Being a player can be a tough thing to let go of. We get it.

You might be surprised by how much we are alike in this. Women love the single years as much as you do—with one big difference. We're not so reluctant to bow out of the game, not as likely to be dragged kicking and screaming into the merger. You, on the other hand, are more like Michael Jordan: It's difficult to retire. We aren't knocking the game—it's great—but eventually, even the best player realizes that if he put as much time and energy into making money or playing sports, he'd be filthy rich or an Olympic athlete.

As a BF, the good news is that you avoid the risk of ending up a fifty-year-old with a fake tan and hair plugs trying to get the twenty-year-old in the corner to show you her tattoos.

You get older, dating gets old. You get tired; it gets tiring; and seducing even the most delicious girl you've ever laid eyes on can get tiresome. Plus, here's the big dirty secret of being a boyfriend: It's fun and a whole new kind of sexy. In the beginning, neither one of you knows whether it will last more than one night, and that can be thrilling. But then you become a couple, and you discover that being your girlfriend turns her on in a whole new way. She's been saving the best for last, and you didn't even know it.

## He Never Saw It Coming

It can happen when you least expect it. There you are, living your life as a free agent, sleeping with this one, flirting with that one, and then, out of nowhere, everything changes. It's that moment when you realize that she has penetrated all your force fields and has reached your inner sanctum. You're caught. She looks at you with those expectant "you're my new boyfriend" eyes and says, "What are we doing next weekend?" or "I can't wait to take you home for the holidays," and before you know it, you're a card-carrying member of the ACLU (Already Claimed Lassoed Up).

Our friend David was a huge player in Chicago. Women were falling out of the trees until one night, when he made his customary moves on a sweet girl named Michelle. He chatted her up, flirted, and got her number. One down. As usual, he continued on to conquests two, three, and four; by the end of the night, his pockets were bulging with small folded pieces of paper. Michelle had watched all this, wasn't threatened by his nonsense, and went up to David and asked for her number back. She very sweetly said, "Let me know when you're ready to stop messing around." That was it. He was hooked. At that moment, despite his worst intentions and his best-laid plans, David fell a little in love. He found his heartstrings being plucked in just the right way at just the right moment. A victim of alchemy, a dedicated player was on the way to being transformed into a dedicated BF. Who knows why Michelle picked David: More to the point, who knows why David didn't run away?

On one hand, you have a choice in the moment she picks you. On the other hand, you don't. This is the perfect BF paradox. A fellow makes a decision not to get into anything serious, then he meets a particular girl, and faster than you can say "weapons of mass destruction," he becomes a BF. It's a perfect mix of chemistry and fate.

## Where Do You Find Her?

Or, perhaps more to the point, where does she find you? Could be anywhere: work, Starbucks, the grocery store, the laundromat, church/temple/mosque, the dog park, the gym. Maybe your sister has a cute friend. Maybe your pals are going to fix you up on a blind date. Or maybe your parole officer can hook you up. The possibilities are endless; that's the good news.

The less than good news is that most women want men

to make the first move. As Horatio said to his buddy Hamlet, "There needs no ghost . . . from the grave to tell us this." (Hamlet, by the way, might have been a classic hero, but he was also a classic shitty BF. First he led Ophelia on, then he denied it. This, as any GF will tell you, is a hell of a way to build a relationship. He drives the poor thing so crazy that she drowns herself in a pond.) But back to you. Making the first move is tough, and we don't envy you. It's a cultural thing, and it's so ingrained that not even the women's movement could inspire us to rethink the notion. We must admit that it's wildly unfair to you guys, but just as we've learned to live with the injustice of high heels, cramps, and butt floss, you're going to have to do most of the pursuing, most of the time.

## BE PREPARED

Every situation is different, so you've got to be prepared. Some girls like grand gestures. That's your aerial game. Others are a little more cautious. That calls for a strong ground game where you grind out short bursts of yardage and try not to fumble. Some girls, well, they seem to keep moving the goalposts. You need every advantage you can get, because this boy-girl thing never takes place on a level playing field. Never.

## *A-Hunting You Will Go*

A lot of potential boyfriends could use some advice in the technique department. As any hunter from Elmer Fudd to Dick Cheney will tell you, don't forget the cardinal rules of the hunt: *Stop, look, and listen.* Put your attention on the quarry, not on your cool gun or handsome orange hunting cap. She might be giving you the green light, but if you're too self-conscious, too busy being cool or showing off your new holster, you're going to miss it. So pay attention. Check her out. Just make sure you're looking at her face, not her breasts. No woman likes to start a conversation by saying "Up here." (Then why is she wearing that shirt?, you may ask. Well, she may want you to notice her boobs, but you'll score big points if you look in her eyes.)

Get familiar with recognizing cues and reading her body language, but bear in mind that sometimes she will feign indifference. How do you tell actual "Leave me alone" indifference from "Here are a few obstacles, let's see what you got" indifference? It can be a fine line. Mistakes can be made. Feelings can be bruised. But still, you've got to try. Has she noticed you? Have you caught her eye as you pass each other in the grocery aisle or while waiting in the ATM line? It's those small moments to take note of. They're fleeting and sometimes subtle, but don't underestimate them, for in this moment she has unlatched the deadbolt and peeked outside, and you have gotten the go-ahead.

In addition to eye contact, here are a few giveaway clues that you are getting over:

- If she runs her fingers through her hair and twirls it, **you're in.**

- If she says you remind her of her father, **you're in.**

- If she seems fascinated with you and keeps asking questions, **you're in.**

- If she goes to the bathroom and comes out wearing more makeup, **you're in.**

- If she laughs at all your jokes, **you're in.**

- If she tells her friends to go ahead without her, **you're unbelievably in.**

## Do You Come Here Often?

Okay, you've read your cues and think that maybe, just maybe, she's receptive to getting to know you a little better. How do you make your move in a gentle, nonthreatening way? While women are receptive to meeting a potential BF in nearly any situation, we are also hardwired to reject the pickup artist. Some things we've heard and never want to hear again:

- Do you work for the post office? Because I could have sworn you were checking out my package.

- The voices in my head told me to come over and talk to you.

- I'll arm-wrestle you for some pussy.

- You can't be first, but you may be next.

- If I said you had a beautiful body, would you hold it against me?

- You had me at hello.

- I seem to have lost my phone number, can I borrow yours?

Meeting someone is hard enough. Save your creativity for the bedroom, not the checkout line. Unless you're Shakespeare, keep it polite, simple, and straightforward. If you're feeling super-confident, you can always slip her your e-mail or your phone number with an easy invitation to contact you. If that feels a little too bold (and every circumstance is different), try some of these gentle (and possibly lame) openers:

- At Starbucks, when the cutie in your sights orders a "venti nonfat no foam light vanilla double-shot cappuccino extra hot," throw out a compliment: *Wow. I admire your stamina.*

- If she is a new neighbor, drop off a box of Krispy Kremes with a short note: *These are great for breakfast, or after a week—when they're nice and stale—they work well as a hammer. If you need anything, just knock.*

- At the dog park, when her Shih Tzu dry-humps your Labradoodle: *I guess love really is blind.*

- At the grocery store as you wait in the ten-items-or-less line: *Will you watch my cart? I forgot Frosted Flakes, and they're the only thing I know how to cook.*

- At the gym, when you're both on the treadmill: *You know, drinking coffee is considered aerobic exercise in most Eastern Bloc countries.*

## The Whole Enchilada

Finally, on the other side of all those things that make being a BF a drag (and yes, it can definitely be a drag) lie those things that most guys want as much as women do. But you can't get one without the other. It's like buying sheets. You may only want the flat sheet—something in a deep masculine stripe—but try as you might, all you can find are sheet sets, so you get stuck with the fitted sheet and a couple of pillowcases to boot.

Okay, that was too girly.

Think of baseball cards: You only want Derek Jeter, but you have to buy the whole pack. Or you only need the 5/16 socket wrench, but they only sell them as a set. To get the thing you actually crave, you have to sign up for the complete package, even though it includes things you never wanted and it costs more than you were planning to spend. In the end, it's pretty great to be with someone who adores you, who makes compromises for you, and who will love having sex with you even when the newness of being a couple has worn off (and you'll find a use for that extra pillowcase). Remember, we have to sign on for the whole package, too. We love you in spite of the fact that not only do you leave little gross hairs in the sink every time you shave, but you love Adam Sandler movies and consider staring at breasts a legitimate pastime. Women aren't likely to invest that kind of patience, support, and love in a player, for the simple reason that a player isn't likely to reciprocate. The only way to get these dividends is to be a boyfriend. Really.

# CHAPTER 3

# BOYMEETSGIRL
# .COM

***So far, the twenty-first century has brought about*** the hybrid car, the perfection of the microprocessor, the end of the Red Sox curse, and the update of the Brawny paper-towel man. It's also seen an explosion of online dating sites. Once the territory of the timid, the desperate, and the witness protection program, online dating sites are now as common as Starbucks—and as popular. No doubt about it, online dating has become the twenty-first-century matchmaker, but instead of an old yenta singing your praises to the girl next door, you get to do it yourself.

If you're set up on a blind date or meet a girl at a bar, it usually takes a couple of dates to get her 411. Meet online, however, and in those first few e-mails you can trade information and make a connection a whole lot faster. Mac or PC? Mormon or Buddhist? Opera box or Xbox? Angelina or Jennifer? What are her hopes and dreams? Is she addicted to prescription drugs, and if so, will she share?

Internet dating sites are like fabulous online catalogs offering a seemingly endless selection of women in every shape, color, and size—from XS to XXL. It's easy to understand the popularity of these sites. You can shop by category,

> With online dating, once you've read her profile, you'll get a sense of who your potential date is. *Former* Playboy *cover girl (Dec. 1995) with a Ph.D. in massage therapy and a massive amount of inherited wealth seeks average Joe who likes to party and doesn't want to be tied down.* Of course, it's possible that she's lying, but don't worry; you'll soon develop a nose for sniffing out the truth. In general, if she sounds too good to be true, she usually is.

find a special style, or just check out the new arrivals. We suggest avoiding the outlet section unless you're going through a dry spell or are hoping for a two-for-one special.

But the Internet offers more than dating speed dial; it can open you up to a world of women you never knew existed. Interested in tugboat maintenance? Underwater basket weaving? Interpretive dance? There's a girl out there for you. Perhaps you'd like to have dinner with a surfer from Bali, or take a hike with a cute refugee who speaks Russian. Or maybe you'd like to connect with a bio-chemist who's into swing dancing and Indian food. Anything is possible.

## Your Wish List

The beauty of Internet dating is that you can do a lot of browsing before you proceed to checkout. Each online dating site caters to a different crowd, so it's a good idea to post on several sites until you find your "people." There are tons of sites out there: Nerve.com, Onion.com, and Salon Personals; craigslist is free, J-Date is for the Chosen People or people who want to be chosen by the Chosen. Still, it's important to ask yourself ~~what you want and what you are ready for.~~ Are you looking to buy or just window-shop?

Most online services will give you many opportunities to declare yourself:

### I am a guy looking for a _____ :

a) casual date
b) serious relationship
c) three-legged beauty queen

Many people will say they are looking for someone open, loving, and funny. And that distinguishes them from exactly no one. Be specific and include as many details as possible. Knowing what you're looking for is key, but equally important is knowing how to articulate it. We have read a lot of profiles in which the "why you should get to know me" is really long and the "what I am looking for" is really short. For example:

**Why you should get to know me:** I might as well be honest and tell you I do stand out from the crowd. I'm fluent in seven languages. I travel the world and pilot my own jet. I am a fun-loving individual. I love sports, opera, and chicken pot pie. My favorite activities are skiing and scuba diving with friends. I am nice to my mother.

**What I am looking for:** A cutie

Sorry, guys, but all this says is that you are self-involved and don't know what you want. It's not sexy, and it's potentially dangerous. So keep it balanced on both fronts.

## First Impressions

You're going to want to say that you make more money than you do, that you're a little cooler, taller, or more sensitive than you are ("I am a billionaire basketball player and take time every day to feel my feelings"). Don't do it. Remember those potato chips they introduced a while back, the ones made with fake fat? You could eat them all day long and not gain an ounce. In reality, everyone who ate them got stomach cramps and explosive diarrhea. They promised one thing and gave you another.

False advertising will ultimately cost you. Be honest but sell your good points. Write from the perspective of a good friend who really knows you and likes you anyway. Mention your character traits, good and bad. "I'm an inveterate liar but great fun at a party." Or "My IQ is room temperature, and bread scares me, but I'm kind to animals and small children." Tell the truth; it's the easiest thing to remember, and your date won't be shocked and disappointed when she meets you at the coffee shop.

Just like a résumé, your online profile offers that crucial first impression. That, plus your initial e-mail to her, translates into thirty seconds (a minute, if you're lucky) of her undivided attention. Use it wisely. Beware of using all capitals: "WHY ARE YOU YELLING AT US?" And remember, the spell-check is your friend. Use it. It's one thing to make spelling errors and quite another to choose not to correct them. Keep your typeface simple—forgo baroque italics or anything over a twelve-point, unless you want to appeal to the large-print set. As for exclamation points—sorry guys, you may think you're expressing your enthusiasm, but when we see !!!!!!!, all we can think is that you're actually a fourteen-year-old girl.

When you send an e-mail to a woman whose profile you like, be specific. Let her know what attracted you to her profile instead of saying only "you sound great." Tell her you like her sense of humor, or that you share her interest in Fellini films or monster-truck racing. If she says "I lived in France for two years," respond with "I spent a month in Paris my junior year" or "I love French bistro cooking, especially cassoulet." Show that you're paying attention. Show that you're interested. And if you've got a wacky sense of humor, by all means indulge it. "I've just had the pleasure of a colonoscopy, and I am good for another ten thousand miles" is a fine rejoinder to "I love the Indy 500."

Online dating is like real estate. You've got to know the code. Every home buyer understands that "cozy" means "cramped," that "partial view" means "dark and depressing," and that "great potential" means "money pit." It's the same with dating. Be a smart shopper. Make sure you understand the lexicon.*

*Animal-loving* ........................*Crazy lady with eighteen cats*

*Healthy and athletic* ..............*Twenty pounds overweight*

*Free spirit* .............................*Slut, wears patchouli*

*My mother would
be horrified* ...........................*Will bring a copy of* Modern Bride *to your first date*

*Caring woman* .......................*Over forty, long braid down her back, bakes banana bread*

*Spunky blonde
who loves Nintendo* ...............*Jail bait, or wizened, bleached, sixty-year-old crazy*

*Laid-back* ..............................*Hasn't worked since she volunteered for McGovern*

*Intelligent is sexy* ...................*Pork-chop ugly*

*Girls just want to have fun* ......*Chunky sorority girl*

*Ciao* ......................................*Uses foreign words, doesn't know the language, a poseur*

*Princess Charming* .................*High maintenance*

*Is chivalry still alive?* ..............*Whiner with a bad track record*

*Don't think we're letting you off the hook, fellas—there is a code that applies to you, too.

## Get the Picture

Peter had a great profile—checked, amended, and approved by a good female friend—but his picture sucked. He superimposed his photo against the background of men landing on the moon. He tinged his face green and even had a thought bubble coming out of his mouth that said, *Need space suit, no oxygen, I'm cold.* Funny? Inventive? Yeah, but also weird. Too weird. Remember: You are part of a long list. It's a display counter, and there is no reason for your potential GF to look at My Favorite Martian when she can scroll down to the Heath Ledger look-alike who's dressed in jeans and a T.

Go for truth in advertising: Use a picture that looks like you, not you ten years and thirty pounds ago, but you today, the best realistic version of you, and one that you like. We recommend having a good friend who happens to have a vagina pick out the photo, or, at the very least, okay it (think of it as marketing research). Once a potential GF has clicked on your profile, then you can get creative, imaginative, and fun.

Our friend Suzanne was e-mailing a guy she really liked, one she felt had great potential. After e-mailing for a while, she sent him a second photo, which was of her on the toilet. You couldn't see anything, but it was a bold choice. She had done something totally in keeping with her sense of humor. She wanted to take a risk and set herself apart from her competition, and she scored! He loved it, and now they are a digit. Be bold. Maybe it won't go over, but if she's not going to laugh at your jokes now, what's the point? Don't waste a lot of time. Next.

## *Your Online Photo*
### *What You Send / What She Sees*

**YOU SEND:** A picture of you and your ex, with her cut out of the picture.

**SHE SEES:** A picture of you and your ex, with her cut out of the picture. Girls hate that.

**YOU SEND:** A hot photo of you shirtless, lying on the bed with your jeans unbuttoned.

**SHE SEES:** Yuck yuck yuck, get it away from me. A guy who loves his body too much and who's gonna take longer to get ready for the date than she does.

**YOU SEND:** A great picture of you and your dog.*

**SHE SEES:** A dog guy, she loves that. So homey.

*\* This does not apply to you and your cat, python, or hamster.*

**YOU SEND:** A picture of you and your BMW, monster truck, Mustang, whatever.

**SHE SEES:** A status-conscious, shallow guy who will no doubt spend his weekends waxing his obsession. And his car.

**YOU SEND:** A picture of your penis. You're proud of it, it looks great, it will turn her on.

**SHE SEES:** The creepiest picture she's ever seen sent by a pervert who is so off-the-charts sick that he actually thinks it's a turn-on.

**YOU SEND:** A great picture of you ten years and thirty pounds ago, hoping that she appreciates your potential.

**SHE SEES:** A great picture of you ten years and thirty pounds ago. And when she meets you for coffee, potential is the last thing she will see.

**YOU SEND:** You looking particularly good in a tux at your best friend's wedding.

**SHE SEES:** A picture of four groomsmen. She can't figure out which one is you, and is attracted to your best friend.

## The Hookup

Once you've made a connection, the e-mailing begins in earnest. Next come the phone conversations, and after those, the first date. All these are vital, but a word of advice: You can get bogged down in any of these steps. Be careful; your fantasy will fill in the blanks that e-mailing and the phone provide.

Our friend Neil made an online connection with a girl from England. They wrote to each other for a long time, then talked on the phone forever. The accent had him hooked, and his fantasy took over. In his mind, he was becoming involved with Keira Knightley. When they met, he saw a pale, reedy woman with bad English teeth and the personality of a tote bag. But because of the Keira Knightley thing, he had signed himself up for dinner and a movie. Every minute was an hour, every hour a day. To top it all off, she liked him and dragged the damn thing out. Neil felt like he was a hostage. And he was: to his imagination.

You also have to watch out for a little matter we'll call "attention versus intention." Some people go online for the attention, even though they have no intention of dating. They're married, they have issues with intimacy, they're nine years old, or maybe ninety-nine. If you really want to meet up with someone, don't spend weeks and weeks investing in a fantasy, or allow yourself to be misled. Be prudent. Cut early. Cut often. Move on.

## *I Thought You'd Be Hotter*

The woman you're connecting with online may seem very different in person. Just because she loves to run and play tennis doesn't mean that she won't be a big girl with a weird walk and a missing arm. Just because she was raised Lutheran and attends church every Sunday doesn't mean that she can't also be the deacon of a satanic cult. Get it?

## Good Luck with That

There are fifty ways to leave your lover (at least), and there are many more ways to get out gracefully before she becomes your lover. Here are a couple to get you started:

- When you're online, say, *Good luck with your . . . novel, small business, puppy mill,* whatever. (Implied: I hope the rest of your life goes well. I know I won't be a part of it.)

- If it's after the first date/coffee, you can send an e-mail with *Thanks for _____; someone is going to be very lucky to find you.* (Implied: It's not going to be me.)

The idea here is that after you've decided to cut bait, do it and do it the right way. Don't just unplug when you want to bow out—you know, "going silent" or "being out of touch." Be a man and tell her you are moving on. This will ensure good karma for you. The online dating genie is watching and likes you to leave the last one in a clean and responsible manner before hooking you up with your next cool date.

## The Proof Is in the Pudding

Your mom was right when she told you not to lick that flagpole. And she was right when she told you that there are a lot of fish in the sea. Nowhere is that more evident than in cyberspace. Little ones, big ones, fat ones, skinny ones, all swimming around inside your computer, waiting to be caught and taken to a movie and then maybe back to your place. We don't advocate online dating over the old-fashioned "Do you come here often" way of meeting people, but it does have a lot of advantages: It's efficient, convenient, and you have more women to choose from. It makes a great supplement, kind of a one-a-day for your social life—but unlike iron, it doesn't leave you constipated.

# CHAPTER 4

# THE FIRST DATE

***Did you ever send letters to Santa when you were a kid?*** We did, and they were longer than that term paper we wrote on the life cycle of the honeybee. The question of what we wanted was important, and we took the time to dream: new bike, drum set, jean jacket, Kirk Cameron pillowcase, New Kids on the Block CD. And just to hedge our bets—no way were we going to get stuck with a Chia Pet—we also included things we might want but weren't entirely sure of: chemistry set, ant farm, little sister, Dad to stop drinking. We took our lists and our letters seriously, and when we mailed them off to the North Pole, we were filled with a sense of excitement and possibility. Something new was coming, and with any luck, it would be something that would make us an even better, cooler, and happier version of ourselves. That feeling is what woke us up at five o'clock on Christmas morning.

Anticipating a first date can be like that. Possibilities abound, things feel thrilling, new, full of potential, and just plain fun. A first date is, after all, a first, and firsts are important. Not only do we get a chance to be with someone new, but we get a chance to be a new version of ourselves as well. That cute girl from work whom you've just asked out will probably spend a lot of time imagining what she'll wear, what she'll talk about, and how she'll feel when she walks into the coffee shop. Most important, she'll spend hours deciding who she wants to be when she's with you: funny girl, mysterious girl, straightforward girl, a guy's girl, demure girl, Powerpuff girl.

Girls carry around a brainful of romantic fantasies, and much of the time, these fantasies will work in your favor. While your date has been out there living her fabulous life and doing all those other things that make her happy, she's also been making her BF wish list and checking it twice. She starts the date already on your side, hoping that you're the present she's been waiting for. She wants you to succeed. So the next time you come down with a major case of nerves before a date, you can make use of this insight, but you don't have to feel obligated by it. If you feel chemistry with her—great. But if you don't, you don't. Sure, she wants you to be The Guy, but at the same time, she's keeping her expectations in check, because she knows that some years you get the Barbie Dream House, and some years you get a wool sweater and socks.

## First Things First

So, the big day arrives, and there you are sharing a bottle of red and an order of fried calamari. Maybe it's an instant success—a love connection—and you like her so much that you wish you could skip the first date and fast-forward to the "we've just had sex, we're a unit, and we're deliriously happy" phase. Or maybe it's a disaster from the moment you arrive and see that she's brought her mother along. Chances are your first date will fall somewhere in between. Women are often reminded that they'll have to kiss a lot of frogs before they find a prince, and the same goes for you guys.

If only there were a *Consumer Reports* that rated candidates and provided testimonials from previous users:

> *She's a beaut . . . makes a crème brûlée that melts in your mouth, and gives a good-night kiss that will curl your toes. Rating (A).* Or: *We cannot recommend this model: loud nasal voice, hates men, and wears jeans below a belly that should have jeans above it. Rating (C–).*

Alas, to our knowledge, no such periodical exists, and thank God, because you wouldn't want to read your rating. And that brings us back to the first-date system. It may be arduous, but it is the most advanced method we have to separate the wheat from the chaff.

## Eight Simple Rules for the First Date (Really Nine)

1. **Show up on time.** Try coming fifteen minutes early, just to be safe. She can be late; you can't.

2. **Keep it short and sweet.** Never have a first date at dinner. If she's not for you *and* a slow eater, you're in the weeds. Think of those construction-paper chains

you made for the Christmas tree when you were a kid: You could always make them longer, but if you wanted to shorten them, you had to rip something.

3. ***Come up with a plan.*** Take it upon yourself to suggest a place you like for coffee or a drink. Take the lead. Most girls will appreciate it if you make a plan so they don't have to.

4. ***Keep it simple, make it fun.*** "I always walk my dog on Sunday mornings. Want to come?" How about a trip to Chinatown to sample those dumplings you can't get enough of. Take turns guessing if that really *was* chicken. Think of the first date as research, an opportunity to collect data to see if there is going to be a second date.

5. ***Invite her into your life.*** Let your date see you in your natural habitat and get a glimpse into your real, "I'm not on a date" life. Show her your neighborhood, your favorite bar, or take her on your favorite hike. Don't take her to the bar where you and your old girlfriend used to hang out unless you are absolutely sure your ex is not going to be there. New prospects like to be invited into your life but not into your last relationship.

6. ***Don't bare your soul.*** "I'm more of a coffee cake guy than a bagel man" is much better than "My mother never breast-fed me."

**7. *Show interest in her life.*** We're not talking about her dreams and aspirations (check out rule number six); this is more on the order of "What's your favorite bad movie?," "What's funnier, a fork or a spoon?," or "What's your secret junk food?"

**8. *Be polite to the person behind the counter.*** Tip well. Your behavior in the world at large tells your date a lot about you. Nothing will end this date faster than bullying the high school kid who is making your latte.

**9. *Don't move too fast.*** You've just met. It's great to be comfortable and be yourself, but throwing your arm around her, nuzzling her forehead, or rubbing her hair is creepy and will make her uncomfortable. Unless she specifically lets you know otherwise, play it safe, and don't do anything beyond a kiss on the first date.

# BE PREPARED

The person you sit down with may not be the person you stand up with. You can begin the date with a tan blond goddess and end it with a gossipy cheerleader who has bad teeth. And the opposite is true, too.

## *Blondes Prefer Gentlemen*

Chivalry may not be dead, but it sure is on life support. That's why being a gentleman in this day and age can really get you points. It's not about being old-fashioned (there's a wide spectrum of behavior between George Clooney and Jack Black); it's about letting your date know that she matters. Open the door for her. Stand up when she comes back to the table. Walk her to her car and wait until she drives away. Offer her your jacket if she's cold. Being a gentleman conveys an attitude of respect for the woman you are with, and the man you are.

Our friend Suzanne set up a drinks date with a guy who was forty minutes late. He came in sweating and chewing gum with the lame excuse that he had trouble finding a

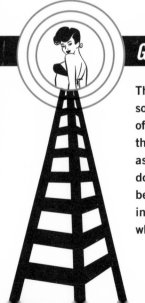

### GPS—*Girlfriend Positioning System*

The first date feels like an audition, which in some ways it is. For many girls, the possibility of not booking the job feels very personal (even though we're auditioning you, too). We take it as rejection rather than as two people who don't have the right chemistry. Maybe it's because tradition tells us it's the guy's job to invite us out, but we always want the offer, whether we want the gig or not.

parking spot. The date went nowhere—no surprise. Suzanne was incredulous when he e-mailed for a second date, and decided to give it to him straight. *You knew I was there and yet you chose to keep me waiting rather than spend $3.50 to valet your car.*

On the other end of the spectrum, our friend Kendall was asked out by a guy who was five-two and looked like a stunt double for Shrek. She wasn't sure she wanted to go out with him and, because women decide everything by committee, even called her sister who runs a yoga studio in Utah. Her sister told her to "keep saying yes to whatever the Universe is offering you" (what do you want, she's a yoga-head), so Kendall said yes. The date was one of the best she ever had. Shrek took her to a fantastic French coffeehouse, was charming, funny, and chivalrous. He picked her up at her apartment (with her consent), opened doors, made sure she was pleased with her cappuccino, double-double-checked that she didn't want a dessert (then we know you don't think we're fat), was amusingly self-deprecating, and even though Kendall wasn't sure about dating the guy, the first date turned into a second and a third and so on. Three weeks later, she also discovered he was hung like a horse and great in bed.

## *First Date*
## *What He Sees / What She Sees*

### *"I'll meet you there . . ."*

*HE SEES:* A hassle-free way of showing up at the restaurant, a way for both parties to keep their options open.

*SHE SEES:* A clueless loner who won't even pick her up. Sure, a lot of women would rather get themselves to the restaurant (car, cab, canoe) and give themselves the chance to make an early exit, but it's the offer that's important here.

### *"Let's go Dutch."*

*HE SEES:* A way to prove he supports women's rights.

*SHE SEES:* A cheapskate who won't spring for a cocktail and obviously doesn't want to see her again.

### *"My ex was such a bitch."*

*HE SEES:* Proof that he is honest and open, not to mention way over his last girlfriend. He doesn't miss her at all and is ready for a new relationship.

*SHE SEES:* A guy who talks trash about his old girlfriend and blames other people for everything. She assumes she'll be next.

### *"Wow, I didn't think you'd be so attractive."*

*HE SEES:* A way to let her know right off the bat that he thinks she's smart and sexy, and he's really excited to be out with her.

**SHE SEES:** A buffoon who talks before he thinks. And why wouldn't I be attractive? Did I sound fat on the phone?

### "Hey, you're actually funny!"

**HE SEES:** An obvious compliment.

**SHE SEES:** An arrogant guy who underestimates her and has appointed himself the arbiter of humor. Who does he think he is, a judge from *Last Comic Standing*?

# True Lies

From the first day you noticed there was more to life than Nintendo, you were sold a bill of goods about girls. The women in your life—your mother, your sisters, your pals who happen to be girls—have all urged you to express your feelings. "If you like a girl," they counsel, "go ask her out." Then high school comes around, and you learn the truth. You take the advice, ask Heather Nicholas out, and she tears down your heart and puts up a cheap motel. In the meantime, shithead Jake—who has never been nice to anyone, anywhere—is getting laid more often than linoleum. What gives?

We know, we know: We're contradicting ourselves. We say, "Let her know early that you want to see her again," and then we say, "Hang back." Both are true. Sorry, we're just the messengers. No one said being a guy was going to be easy.

## *Too Cool, Too Eager, or Just Right?*

A lot of men think women, children, and small animals are a lot alike: If you want them to come to you, don't go to them. Let's say you have a first date and you really like her. You like her so much, you don't want to blow it by being too eager. So you go to the other extreme and are too cool. You don't call her for a week. Or you invite her to a party like this: "A bunch of us are going for a drink, you can come if you want." But being too cool invites your potential GF to respond by dusting off her collection of insecurities: "Oh God, he doesn't like me. Oh God, he doesn't think I'm smart enough. Oh God, he hasn't called me." She does this in the privacy of her own home and to her girlfriends. What you're forgetting is that while "too cool" may have worked in third grade, it stopped being effective in fifth.

Unfortunately, "too eager" doesn't work well, either. Our friend Lena was flirting with a guy online and was just about to make the first coffee date. He jumped the gun and got their compatibility astrology charts done and put together a Photoshop composite of what their children would look like before they even met. (Oh—there's also something called too much, too late. Isabel ran afoul of this on her sixth date with a cinematographer when he informed her he was actually a DP for porn.)

Happily, there is something just right, and this is what it looks like: Susan went on a great first date with a guy she was really attracted to. He left her place around midnight and called her twenty minutes later to say he had a great time. Enthusiastic? Yes. Too eager? No. In the words of Goldilocks, it was just right.

When you don't know what to do on the too cool/too eager question, put your attention on her. What do you see? Not what you'd like to see, or hope to see. What do you actually see in front of you? Is she enjoying the date, or is she just being polite and a good sport? Is she engaged in the conversation, asking questions and offering up stories, or is she just listening to you? Has she ordered another drink, or is she slowing down and possibly thinking about leaving? Checking out her nails or playing with her rings could be a sign she is distracted. So is yawning, checking her BlackBerry, or updating her résumé. If you really can't tell—and we know it's tough sometimes—ask her. We mean it. "This has been really fun, I'm having a great time. I'd like to see you again. Why don't I call you tomorrow after you've checked your schedule?" (The schedule thing is important because it has a built-in out for her. When you call the next day, she can blame it on her schedule, and you can get the message.)

## We Must Do This Again Sometime

Your potential GF (if she's into you) will want to know at the end of the date whether you're interested. So tell her. It's thrilling to hear "I'd love to see you again." It makes our hearts pound and our imaginations soar—we may still be standing on the doorstep, but in our minds, we're rushing out to buy new panties. Calling the next day works well, too. A guy who knows what he likes and says it is a big turn-on. Remember that: It has big payoff potential for dates number two and three (think sex).

If the date was a bust, you'll probably both know it, and once you drop her off, you are free to move on with the rest

## BE PREPARED

**TEN THINGS YOU SHOULD NEVER SAY ON THE FIRST DATE:**

1. You look a lot like my mother.*

2. You look a lot like my ex-girlfriend.*

3. You can walk from here.

4. I just did that to freak you out.

5. I'm thinking of swans. They mate for life.

6. Your nose looks like your friend's, but hers is fatter.

7. You have beautiful legs; they'd look great wrapped around my neck.

8. I can tell you're not fat 'cause of your arms.

9. Sorry, I'm a little out of it, I have a sex hangover.

10. I love this place, I just brought a date here yesterday.

*\* Basically, the "you look a lot like" observation should be avoided at all costs, unless the look-alike is on the cover of this month's FHM.*

of your life. The good news is that if the date really sucked, you'll be reminded of all the great things about being single: You get to eat where and when you want, keep the television on as loud as you like, and spend your time how you jolly well please, watching sports, visiting strip clubs, scrapbooking . . . whatever.

# CHAPTER 5

## WHEN DO YOU BECOME A BOYFRIEND, AND WHO DECIDES?

*She does.*

# CHAPTER 6

# DO I LOOK FAT?

**Imagine your girlfriend is hanging out at your apartment.** The two of you are cozy on your naugahyde couch, relishing this moment of togetherness, the casual intimacy of an evening spent with a couple of DVDs and a bottle of wine. It's perfect, a twenty-first-century Eden, with take-out menus and a flat-screen TV. And then she picks up your copy of the *Sports Illustrated* swimsuit issue. "What do you think of *her*?" she asks, her voice dripping with innocence and laced with danger. The "her" in question is the sexiest supermodel you've ever seen. Slightly sandy, moist from the surf in a buckskin Band-Aid-size bikini (with fringe), she seems to be looking right at you. Looking right through you, in fact, right through your favorite Coldplay T-shirt and into the depths of your very soul.

HOLD IT RIGHT THERE.

Take a deep breath. Avoid any sudden movements. You'll need to move fast, but you can't sacrifice accuracy for speed. Choose your response carefully. Make sure every word is distinct and clear. And whatever you do, don't say the first thing that comes to mind. That's the mark of an inexperienced BF, and it could lead you down the road to ruin.

Inappropriate responses—otherwise known as *Now you're fucked*:

- "Damn, she's hot."
- "Hang on—let me get my glasses."
- "How come *I* never meet those kind of girls?"
- "Come to Papa."

Appropriate responses—otherwise known as *You're the man*:

- "She's beautiful, but I like your body better."
- "Oh God, those girls are scary."
- "She's too thin, and her boobs are too big . . . yuck."
- "It's all been airbrushed anyway."

You don't need to know Morse code to decipher the not-so-secret language at work behind your GF's seemingly harmless question. She wants reassurance, pure and simple. So handle with care. Even if she doesn't believe your kind words, she'll sure appreciate the loyalty.

## Losing It

Before you get to such questions as "Do you love me" or—shudder—"What do you think of this china pattern?," you will have to traverse the danger zone of "Do I look fat?" This question, like too much coffee, can leave you wired, on edge, and grinding your teeth if you are not prepared for it. Get ready. This is no ordinary chat.

"Do I look fat?" will come up in various forms. Sometimes it will be specific: "Do I look fat in this dress?" Or generic, such as "How do I look?" It can be disguised as a statement: "I feel fat" or "I'm so fat I could date myself." Unless you're looking for a convenient, albeit spectacular, way of breaking up, the answer to any form of this question can never be "Yeah, you do look a little chunky."

Losing weight is a project for men; for women it's an obsession. Our friend Kevin was complaining about his love handles. In truth, the guy was up thirty pounds. Kevin, like most guys, had a lot more wiggle room in this area. He also had a really cute GF and a great self-image. For him, losing weight was just another item on his to-do list, like "I'm going to clean out the garage" or "I'm going to build a deck."

If your GF wants to lose twenty pounds, she'll need a support group, a weekly meeting, a new notebook, a juicer, weight-loss magazines, power-yoga videos, inspirational DVDs, and a lot of sugarless gum. That's just for starters. What guy do you know who would go out in a snowstorm with wet hair and no shoes, hoping to get sick and drop a few pounds? What guy do you know who would take a few bites of his delicious dinner and then dump Sweet'n Low and vinegar on it just to make sure he won't eat the rest? What guy do you know who would eat an Ex-Lax cracker sandwich just to fit into an old pair of jeans? What guy do you know who would keep a bottle of ipecac in his purse, just in case he overeats?

The truth is, we women are so obsessed with our bodies that we often rate our experiences according to how much we weigh or how we feel about the shape we're in. Looking back over snapshots of vacations, we think, "Oh yeah, I was a hundred and twenty pounds then, that was a good trip." Or, conversely, "Oh God, I was so fat on that vacation to the Grand Canyon, it was the worst trip." It doesn't matter whether we are exploring Mayan ruins, sightseeing in Paris, or having a wild weekend with our girlfriends in Las Vegas, and it doesn't matter how much fun we had; it all pales in comparison to our body image at the time. We could go to our grave obsessing about twelve pounds—and we're not kidding. If we could put down our obsession, we could use all that effort and energy to help save the world. Or, at the very least, remember our vacations for where we went, what we did, and who we met—not how we looked. Unfortunately, we don't grow out of this, so we have to overcome it. All we ask from you is patience. Just because we waste our time entangled with the issue doesn't mean you have to.

> **When guys have a gut, they rub it affectionately and give it a nickname. No woman has ever named her thighs.**

## *Body Language*

Consider it from our point of view. Perfectly proportioned, stunningly beautiful, nearly nude women are everywhere you look, on billboards, in magazines, and on TV. But just because these images are everywhere doesn't mean they go down easy. What's eye candy to you is a kick in the stomach to us. Advertisers aren't stupid. They know we're all drawn to the language of sex. Women are drawn to it because we're masochists. Men are drawn to it because of the fantasy and the possibility—however remote—of turning fantasy into reality. We get it. We're not looking to change your reaction and, unfortunately, after years of therapy, we still can't change ours.

## GPS—*Girlfriend Positioning System*

Did you know that a girl has to spend half an hour speed walking to burn as many calories as her BF does watching thirty minutes of football sitting in his Barcalounger? Turns out that little thing called testosterone not only makes you good at reading maps, it makes your body a calorie-burning machine. Damn you. Besides the physiology, which works in your favor, the playing field isn't level out there. Women can never be too thin or too pretty. Talk about pressure (you try passing cellulite off as a cool little addition to your ass). Skinny girls worry about looking fat, and fat girls worry about looking fat. Why do you think women are so into shoes? Because they always fit.

## *You Are Who You Eat*

Chances are, you will never see your GF exhibit her full range of insane food behaviors. (Remember, we try to "keep crazy in the bottle" so we don't scare you off.) But here are some behaviors you may observe that we can decipher for you.

*The Starbucker.* If she's drinking six cups of coffee at a sitting, your GF is probably a Starbucker who is trying to avoid food. Sooner or later, she'll break down and eat, and then you'll have a wired, bloated, cranky woman on your hands. If you're dating a Starbucker, try to slip her some bread. It will soak up the caffeine and mellow out the highs and lows.

*The Night Eater.* She can go through the entire day on a LUNA bar, but once darkness comes, your Night Eater will inhale everything in sight. Worse, come morning, she'll end up with a food hangover, which means she'll feel like she's moving underwater with a couch tied to her back (this would be her ass). You wouldn't wake a sleepwalker, and you shouldn't confront a Night Eater, especially when morning comes around.

*The "Nothing for Me, Thanks" Girl.* Very similar to the Night Eater in that she will be cranky and short-tempered because she hasn't eaten all day, the "Nothing for Me, Thanks" Girl can binge (two hot dogs, three bananas, two packages of Weight Watchers mac and cheese, the rest of your little brother's birthday cake, and a Diet Coke) at any time, in any place, which is why her mood swings rival any theme-park ride. If you're dating this girl, try offering her a bite of your apple or a sandwich. Toss bar nuts into her mouth, anything to keep her blood sugar up.

**The Grazer.** Like a horse, the Grazer eats standing up. She can usually be spotted by the kitchen counter, moving listlessly from one cabinet to the next, with her hand in a box of Triscuits. If this describes your GF, try not to surprise her while she's grazing. If you do, pretend you have seen nothing out of the ordinary.

**The Garbage Grubber.** See a pair of high heels and clean-shaven legs sticking out of the trash can? Then you've spotted a Garbage Grubber. The GG's natural habitat is the hilly territory of remorse and resolve. She eats ice cream, feels bad about it, then throws half the carton away. Fifteen minutes later, she's rooting around in the garbage, picking up said carton, and eating three more bites until she throws it away again in disgust. If you catch your GF in the act of garbage grubbing, carefully maneuver around her and break the pattern by gently taking out the trash.

Our advice to you? Steer clear of the whole food thing. Don't note what your GF eats (or doesn't) or how often she eats (or doesn't). Let her handle it. We know some of you guys are saying, "But that is all she talks about. How can I steer clear of something I hear about 24/7?" You're right. You can't. So tell her. Tell her you can't hear about it all the time and she'll have to come up with some other topic of conversation. Make sure to tell her you love her anyway. Then pass her a cookie (just kidding).

## Love the One You're With

Our friend Larry was dating a lovely girl who happened to be a size fourteen. They had everything in common: horses, outdoors, guns, Rush Limbaugh, great sex, and conversation. They were a terrific match. But at their engagement party, Larry turned to his future brother-in-law and said, "I know she's a little chunky now, but once we're married, things will change. I like my girls skinny." Well, they got married, and Cynthia stayed a size fourteen, except when she was a size sixteen. This is not a story about Larry being an asshole. This is a story about Larry being thickheaded. Don't sign up for what you don't see in front of you. We mean it. If you keep thinking to yourself or saying to your buddies,

## BE PREPARED

Love up her body the way you find it, or find a body that you can love up—and remember, at some point you will begin to go bald, and we will be kind.

> **Fair's fair.** If you have a GF who keeps coaching you on what to eat and nudging you to the gym or complaining about *your* love handles, tell her you're pretty sure you signed up for a girlfriend, not a trainer, coach, or critic.

"Yeah, but if she'd lose five, ten, fifteen [fill in the blank] pounds, she'd be really hot," then one of three things is happening:

- You've signed up for the wrong girl.

- You don't like the way real women are shaped.

- You're gay.

She's not going to lose the weight for you, no matter what. And if you try to force the issue—as in "You really want that second brownie, honey?"—her feelings will be hurt *and* she'll feel bad about herself around you. Translation, fellas: *No nookie.*

Don't believe us? Consider our friend Suzanne. She was sitting on the couch with her boyfriend, watching TV, when he lay down and put his head in her lap. She immediately got self-conscious about her tummy—she knew he could feel how soft it was, how much it stuck out. Suzanne tried to suck it in, but forty minutes into *Grey's Anatomy*, she forgot, and much to her horror the pooch pooched out. And then her BF did a remarkable thing. He reached around, rubbed her stomach, and said, "Baby, I love your curves, I love how soft you are. Relax." They were naked before the next Lunesta commercial.

## *Body of Knowledge*

There is no aphrodisiac as powerful as a boyfriend who loves a real woman's body: the curves, the softness, the fat part, the thin part, the bumps, the hair, the smell—the real deal.

To truly understand the question "Do I look fat?," you must understand that it isn't really a question. Your GF isn't asking for your honest opinion; she's asking for reassurance. So, how *do* you respond to "Do I look fat?" One word: No. If you have to lie, then lie. It's that simple. The answer is always, unfailingly, unhesitatingly, undeniably *no! Nope. Naw. No way. Non. Nein. Nee.*

# CHAPTER 7

# YOUR CALL IS IMPORTANT TO US

***Let's cut to the chase. Your girl-
friend is going to want*** you to call her. A
lot. And once she's got you on the phone, she's going to want
to talk. A lot. For a long time. Twenty minutes may be an
eternity for you, but for your girlfriend, it's a warm-up.
Training since she was twelve, she has built up the endurance
of a marathon runner. While you were spending your time
playing Sega Genesis, she was honing her skills at talking
about nothing for hours. She can kick your ass in this event,
which is a shame, because chances are you don't even want to
be in the competition.

We don't know any men who like to chat. Do you?

Men use the phone to give and receive pertinent information. Women use the phone as a way to bond, and we
can't imagine that you're not going to use it in this way, too.
Your GF will want to experience your day through your conversation (and vice versa) as a way to be close. She wants to
know how you are. The inside stuff—not merely the results.
Your girlfriend will take your "yes," "no," "good," "bad" conversation as a rejection even if you don't mean it that way.

Can you get out of talking on the phone? No. Not really.
Men have tried for decades to figure out how, without much

success; however, a few simple adjustments to the way you approach the issue should keep her happy and keep you sane.

## Rollover Minutes

It's not just that women like to talk on the phone more than men, although they do. And it's not just that women like to divulge more personal information than men, although they do. Men interrupt—please let us finish—more than women do. And women ask more questions than men do. (You didn't know that?) And as if that weren't enough, men are more direct in their conversation, more likely to make bold statements. Women, on the other hand, are more likely to be concerned with how the person on the other end of the phone is doing. It's not that one of us is right and the other is wrong; it's that we have different ways of doing things. This shouldn't come as a surprise. When's the last time you saw your girlfriend drinking milk straight from the carton?

The thing is, you can get credit for staying in touch, being attentive, thoughtful, considerate, and loving, all without leaving the comfort of your Bluetooth. With a very small investment—say a two-minute conversation—you can reap a substantial return. The calls can be short, but you score major points by phoning her two or three times a day. Follow this advice, and you can avoid that hour-and-a-half "Do you love me?" conversation at the end of a long day. Think of it as the premium you pay to keep your relationship insurance current.

We can tell you're scratching your head on this one. "How in the world do I have a brief conversation with a woman? Just trying to give my mom flight information turns into a twenty-minute chat." These perfectly respectable, minimally sneaky solutions should do the trick:

- Call when you know you won't reach her. "I know you're not home, but I was thinking about you and what a great time we had at the art exhibit/hot-dog-eating contest/evening of lesbian poetry/[insert your last date here]."

- Call when you have only two minutes to spare. "Hey, I gotta go into a meeting in a second, but I needed a [insert GF name here] fix. How are you?"

- Call when you know she'll be busy. "I think you're getting ready for your ten A.M. appointment, but got a second to catch up? I just wanted to say hi." (You'll win bonus points for remembering she *has* a ten A.M. appointment.)

- Call to ask a quick question. "Does your sister like candles or should I just get her a CD for her birthday? Could you give it some thought?" This one has the added advantage of connecting over something real. It's a bonding moment, and your GF will know that you value her input. (Also, hello? You're buying a present for her sister? You rock. We give you permission to throw this book away.)

When used as directed, these tactics are 93 percent effective. Still, you're going to need assistance for that other 7 percent of the time. We can help there, too. If you find your GF going on longer than you'd like, you can always wrap up the call by bookending your getting-off-the-phone reasons with sweet talk, as in "I love talking to you, but I'm just . . . finishing this report/turning on to the interstate/donating a kidney/[insert your reason here], thanks for being so cool about it." When you bookend—and we're claiming it as a verb—you give your girlfriend what she needs while backing her into being understanding.

## Hold the Phone

Talking on the phone is like flossing. You keep your teeth and your GF a lot longer if you do both. And just like that dental hygienist who always wants to review proper flossing

**GIRL ON GIRL**
*Advice for Your Girlfriend!*
........................................

Men will never use the phone the way you do. Once they've told you what time they want to pick you up and where you are having dinner, they are ready to hang up. The only time you will get your boyfriend to have long intimate phone conversations with you is before he is your boyfriend.

technique, we can offer some tried-and-true methods to keep plaque (and other assorted gunk) from collecting between you and your better half.

- When you tell us you're going to call on a particular day or at a particular time, don't mess around—CALL. Please don't underestimate the importance of this. It really matters to us.

- If we call you at a bad time (you're working, you're watching TV, you're exfoliating), tell us you can't talk and that you'll call us back. Otherwise we chase you around verbally, not knowing why you're distracted, worried it's something we did, and the conversation gets weird and fucked up.

- For big, big points, ignore your call waiting, and take credit for it: "I don't want to talk to anyone but you."

- If you have caller ID, don't avoid her calls too many times, or else make sure she doesn't find out you were home screening.

And be honest: Have you ever been talking to your GF on the phone and staring into the mirror? Guess what—we can hear you studying yourself. We hear your voice change slightly, and we can feel your mind wandering away from the conversation and into the fascinating world of "Is that a blackhead? Do I need to shave? Is my hairline receding? Jesus, I'm cute." Yep, you're a multitasker, but the gig is up. We can tell when you are talking to us and madly e-mailing, going over paperwork, or watching the game (see chapter on television). We just wanted you to know.

P.S.: If you have to pee while talking to us, pee on the side of the bowl so we won't hear the splashing; and if you have to poop, we'd rather you call us back after you are done.

## Static on the Line

Although it can be easier to say "I love you" on the phone than in person (in fact, it's the only place our friend Lou can say it), it's also easier for conversations to spin out of control and quickly degenerate into long, sticky relationship discussions. These discussions, which always seem to happen in the middle of the night, are deadening. You don't need directory assistance to find your way out of the conversation and into bed; all you need is a simple: "This is too important, let's wait till we see each other." This kind of statement will calm your girlfriend. She'll know you aren't blowing her off, and you can get some shut-eye.

## BE PREPARED

When we break up with someone—or more often, when he breaks up with us—we call him to see if he's home. If he answers, we hang up, then we call back a couple hours later. Or we tap in to his voicemail. We're not proud of it, but we can't help ourselves. So if there is anything you don't want us to hear, delete it immediately. Better yet, change your access code.

If you do get into a fight on the phone, always end the conversation with kindness, a word of caring or love. Say it even if it feels like a lie and you hate your GF at that moment, because the fact is, eighteen hours later, you will love her again, and in the meantime, she'll really appreciate the gesture. It's a hedge for the future.

## *You've Got Mail*

It seems like e-mail was invented with the BF in mind. It's the perfect forum for a quick flirt and a great secret weapon if you want to avoid a phone conversation. E-mail feels like intimacy without all the intimacy. Genius. It's one of the easiest, most painless ways to connect, and your GF will love it. There's nothing better than getting a quick e-mail from your guy. It can be short and sweet—"How's your day going?"; or a little more provocative—"Are you wearing the red thong? I just had a feeling you were."

E-mail is also a great way to make up after a fight. A quick "I'm sorry" or "I'm a bonehead, let's start over" really clears things up. Best-case scenario, the e-mail will put the fight to bed. But if she still needs to talk about it (and she might), at least you've done the hard part the easy way—apology in absentia.

Remember, while it saves you from the phone call (which is over when it's over), an e-mail is forever. The problem with any paper trail is that it's a paper trail. If it is a really good e-mail or a really bad one, she will forward it to her friends and maybe even her shrink.

## *Take a Letter*

The phone has its place; e-mails, too. But there's nothing like a letter. A letter is like a secret, a quiet conversation between just the two of you that no one else even knows about. It's romantic and old-fashioned, and she can keep it in her jewelry box or lingerie drawer.

When our friend Julie was in eighth grade, she got a letter from her boyfriend who was away at camp. He drew a picture of two stick figures standing next to each other and under it wrote, *Aren't we cute together? Love, Andy.* She's thirty and still has it. Unlike a present that you buy for us, a letter is actually a little piece of you, your handwriting, your spelling, your spit on the envelope (or to the criminally minded, your DNA).

A letter doesn't have to be clever or witty. Just leave it on the kitchen counter: *Ate the rest of the birthday cake for lunch, wasn't bad. Thinking of you.* Little letters or notes (Post-its are acceptable) left lying around or sent through snail mail are a

## BE PREPARED

If you've screwed up and been out of touch, don't try to cover by blaming it on the technology. We GFs will never buy the "didn't you get my e-mail?" routine. Dogs don't eat homework, and e-mails don't go missing like socks in the dryer.

perfect and painless way to connect. Two sentences can pack a wallop. Let a girl know you are looking forward to dinner tonight, and she's halfway undressed.

We pay attention to your letters in a different way than we do to your e-mails or phone calls. Maybe it's because they don't come around that often. Whatever the reason, be aware that a letter carries weight. Use this to your advantage. You can break up with someone in a letter, but only a weenie breaks up in an e-mail, and only a coward breaks up on a Post-it. (Your GF remembers that *Sex and the City* episode, even if you don't.)

## Can You Hear Me Now?

Keeping in touch can be a delight or a drag. If you find yourself limply capitulating to your GF's demands for phone time, instant messaging, or even letters, stop. E-mail and the telephone can be a burden, just another thing you have to "get right" for your girlfriend, or they can be a secret weapon in your arsenal of romance and seduction. Turn an enemy into a friend. Think of them as a means to an end, like foreplay. The trick is to make the connection in a way that satisfies you both. When you change your perception, you change your experience. Wasn't there a time when you thought girls had cooties?

# CHAPTER 8

# MONEY

***Our friend Jane was skiing with her boyfriend,*** and he kept pointing out cute ski bunnies. It was meant to be funny and kind of a joke, and she tried to be a good sport about it, but finally, she had enough. "Hey," she said, "do you want me to start pointing out guys who are more successful than you?" Point taken. He got it, and we want you to get it. Money is for a man what beauty is for a woman: power and status and a backstage pass to any show you want to see. It's the difference between a high-speed connection and dial-up. The pressure women feel to be young, gorgeous, and thin is crushing. Men are operating under the same pressure, except it's pressure to have money and be successful.

We admit it, a rich guy is a turn-on for women. That girlfriend icon Carrie Bradshaw didn't fall for Mr. Little, did she? A guy with money looks like the answer, just the way a gorgeous woman looks like she's all you need, the yellow brick road to happily ever after. This doesn't mean rich men make the best boyfriends; often they are entitled assholes who think of nothing but money. But money is sexy.

Some women are obsessed with it, for others it's just a nice bonus. If you're loaded, you may get our attention, but it won't be enough to steal our hearts. We know you're scoffing—hear us out. Obviously, we'll get turned on when you fly us to St. Barth's on your platinum G5, but if you're a humorless boor, even that lifestyle will lose its luster pretty quickly, because the truth is, most women care about money, just not for the reasons that you think.

If you make a good living, we'll find that attractive, partly because of the freedom and stability money can bring. But the deeper draw will be what that money represents. We see a guy who has some money, and unless he's burning through a trust fund (which is fine, by the way; we'll help), it says that he's responsible, that he's good at what he does, that he takes care of business. And that speaks to his character, which is hot in a way that doesn't fade. Just so there's no confusion, we're not saying you have to be rich. We'll be equally impressed by the generous and responsible use of more moderate means. For most of us, it's not the size of your bankroll but how you use it that counts.

## *Dating and Dollars*

It used to be easy. Men paid and women said thank you. Men also wore hats, and women wore gloves and chiffon scarves. But the rules aren't so clear anymore, and men and women are often confused by the etiquette of dating and money. It's more than who pays and how much. The way you deal with money can reveal who you are and how you feel about the person you are with. Money represents another form of intimacy, and you have to be aware of that. And like that other, more popular form of intimacy—S-E-X—you need to know that the rules for dating are not the same as those for a bona fide couple.

- ***Don't forget your wallet.*** In the beginning, unless your date expressly asks to go Dutch (this does not mean wooden shoes and funny hats), assume that you're paying. It may seem old-fashioned, and maybe one day it will change, but at this point that's the rule.

- ***Don't get carried away.*** Generosity is appealing, but don't overextend yourself. Stay within your comfort zone. If you keep spending beyond your means, she'll assume those are your means, then you'll resent her, and she'll have no idea why.

- ***Don't be a chauvinist.*** If your girlfriend wants to take you out, be gracious. Don't insist on paying for cotton candy, tattoos, circus tickets, [insert expenditure here]. You want to be modern but chivalrous.

- ***Don't be cheap.*** Never, ever itemize the bill. If it matters to you that her tofu fajitas cost two dollars more than your chicken parmesan, you should have stayed home.

- ***Don't expect something for your money.*** It's not quid pro quo. Buy her dinner when you want to buy her dinner, not when you want a blow job. (Fellatio for fettuccine is an insult to you both.)

- ***Don't stiff the waiter.*** If you see your date giving the waiter an "I'm sorry" look, you're not tipping enough. A minimum of fifteen percent is standard, and you should factor that in to the price of the evening.

- ***Don't use coupons.*** Honestly, do you really need that free beverage or complimentary entrée of greater or lesser value?

## *Material Girls*

We've all seen women who are Trump hunting, trolling the seas for a guy with big bucks who can hoist them onto his lap of luxury. Problem is, some of these women are tantalizingly gorgeous. But even if you've got the wad to get their attention, steer clear, because if they oohed and ahhed over your Benz, chances are they will hop right out when a Bentley pulls up.

### *Romeo on a Budget*

You don't have to be Howard Hughes to take her on a date that will knock her socks off. Most of the time, what you do together is less important than the spirit with which you carry it off. Our friend Shawn, a talented but perennially starving NYC musician, had a slam dunk deal-closer date that consisted of hot dogs off a cart followed by a sunset ride on the Staten Island ferry. The skyline was gorgeous, the idea of sharing a unique view of the city he loved was romantic, and the whole thing set him back about $4.95. Sure, it scared off some dates, but the truth is, they wouldn't have stuck around anyway.

## Great Cheap Dates

- **Get sweaty.** Take her biking, hiking, or walking. If she's so inclined, take her to the batting cage.

- **Ants in her pants.** A picnic may sound corny to you, but it probably won't to her. Find out what she likes to eat and then surprise her with it in a basket.

- **Cult classic.** Host your own private film festival. Share your favorite old movies all night in the coziness of your own bed. Choose wisely, though; not every girl will find the *Terminator* trilogy as hot as you do.

- **Keep a light on for her.** Have an afternoon rendezvous at Motel 6. Bring quarters to make the bed jiggle. But don't make this a regular thing, or it'll turn sleazy faster than you can say "lousy thread count."

- **That's amore.** Grab a Louis Prima CD, a bottle of wine, and cook Italian at your place. Make sure to get the good stuff. She'll recognize Beefaroni even if she doesn't see the can.

- **Spa night.** Give her a pedicure, including polish. It'll be sexy even if you do a bad job. And you will.

- **Killing spree.** Pretend she's a guy and take her to the video arcade for an evening of annihilation.

- **Early-bird special.** Pretend you're old folks and sit on a bench in the park, then take her to an afternoon movie. No porn unless she suggests it.

- **Daydream believers.** Go window-shopping in the chic section of town. Fantasize about what life will be like when you hit the big time. Stop for overpriced coffee and a slice of pie.

If she's half the girl we think she is, she'll love the thought you put into these dates and respect you for living within your means. But there's a very important addendum: When your ship comes in, even if it just docks for the weekend, take her out and live a little. Spring for a concert, a show, maybe dinner at the place everyone's talking about. If you've been living Motel 6, tonight's the night you spring for the Ritz. You'll have a great time, and without having to say much, show her how much you appreciate her willingness to play within your boundaries.

## When You're an Item

Okay, time has passed, and now you're a couple. Congratulations, and welcome to the BF club. Now you have some-

# *Baby Got Greenbacks*

So your new girlfriend's loaded. A vagina and money? You scored. Right? Well, it's not always that simple. The good news is you don't have to support her, and she's probably not after you for your money. The bad news is that while you're having a great time tagging along to her beach house every weekend, your inner caveman is gradually being relieved of his core duties. Deprived of providing food and finding shelter, he starts to feel like a bimbo in loincloth. That makes him mad. And when inner caveman gets mad, he acts out. Lamps get broken, couches get slept on. And that's not fun for anyone. So, what do you do? Negotiate an arrangement that you're both comfortable with, so that you can feel like a man and she doesn't have to completely abandon the lifestyle she's accustomed to. If, after searching your heart, you find that you can't date an heiress without feeling bad about yourself, fine. But before you bail, make sure she takes you shopping.

one to call when you get that great job or promotion, and someone to bitch to when that knucklehead puts a ding in your Harley. Why do you suddenly find yourself with these options? Because you have a GF. And that will alter the way you deal with each other when it comes to money, in both subtle and not so subtle ways.

It's a good idea to lay out some ground rules so that everyone has an equal stake in the partnership. Here are a few tips to help you navigate this new terrain.

- **Can't buy me love.** Don't substitute money for attention. Taking her somewhere nice or buying lavish presents is no substitute for spending relaxed, undistracted time with your focus placed squarely on her.

- **Thanks for sharing.** Your new position in her life may make you feel you have the right to criticize the way she spends money, especially when she blithely tosses out the shocking number she just spent on a pair of shoes. Don't do it. She wants you to say that she's worth that and more. (When you do, odds are she will model those shoes so that you can view them without the distraction of clothes or undergarments.)

- **Bossy boots.** If you are paying most of the bills, don't use that as leverage or think your disproportionate financial contribution makes your voice louder than hers when it comes to making decisions. This is the arrangement you signed up for, and you want her to feel like an equal partner. So stick to the deal. Nobody likes a player who tries to renegotiate his contract in the middle of the season.

- **It's not in the budget.** As the relationship progresses, you will find you have to start planning together—vacations, big purchases. Don't be afraid to do a little informal financial planning with her. Nothing too revealing or uncomfortable, simply a way of organizing your shared dreams and priorities. This will give you something to look forward to and show her you are capable of considering next year with her in it. If she occasionally succumbs to exorbitant impulse buys (we heard some women do this), your previously stated targets will give you a gentle, loving framework to help her reconsider that Prada dog carrier.

## The Shift

When she turns thirty or so, your girlfriend—who has until now been perfectly happy watching reruns of *Seinfeld* and eating mac and cheese in your apartment—will all of a sudden start talking about real estate, your careers, and IRAs. Relax. This doesn't mean she's become materialistic; it means she's really into you and is willing to consider a future with you, as long as it's not in a trailer. We know even the word "future" makes your package wilt a little, because a part of you has been clinging to the fantasy that this phase might go on forever. It won't. The *Seinfeld* and the mac and cheese will stay the same, but unless you hook up with a steady GF, chances are you will share these goodies with a parade of increasingly skanky and more pathetic girls until even they desert you, and your mother dies of a broken heart. So if you want to avoid killing off dear old Mom, you have to ask yourself two questions.

1. Am I ready to start thinking about real estate, my career, and IRAs?

2. Am I ready to start thinking about those things with her?

If the answer to both is yes, then great. If you're not ready, tell her. She may decide to give you more time, and you'll get to spend it in the far more pleasant realm of mutual respect and honesty. If you are ready for all that but not with her, tell her that, too. When she gets over her hurt feelings, she will think of you (accurately) as a stand-up guy. In the meantime, you will have freed yourself up for the right woman, who may be around the very next corner. Whatever you do, don't fake it, because when she finds out where you really stand, she'll be twice as pissed at you, and she'll be justified.

## Show Me the Money

In the same way that women have a hard time believing men can love anything other than a perfect body, men seem to have trouble accepting that women can want someone of quality over quantity. Yes, diamonds are a girl's best friend, until the day the girl gets the flu, and then her best friend, regardless of his net worth, is the guy with the chicken soup and a copy of *When Harry Met Sally*. So don't sweat it if you're not Donald Trump (and we hope you're not, for so many reasons, not the least of which is bad hair). Your girl-friend knows the price of highlights and the value of a dollar, and she knows the worth of a good guy, too. So if you are picking her up in your junky Toyota, stand tall, my friend. Great BFs also arrive by bus.

# CHAPTER 9

# YOUR PLACE OR MINE?

***Once upon a time, in the long-ago 1960s, a hunky astronaut***—let's call him Major Cutie—found a bottle on a deserted beach. Miles away from the nearest bar and in desperate need of a drink, he uncorked it. And there she was: a gorgeous woman with a serious rack, a long blond ponytail, and the wardrobe of a stripper. He took her home (wouldn't you?) and thus began their happy new life together.

*I Dream of Jeannie* ran for years for the simple reason that it portrayed a collective fantasy. He comes home to a scantily clad blonde who's crazy in love with him, calls him "Master," and isn't a bad cook. With no hard feelings, she disappears when necessary, into her magic bottle, which looks a lot like a love nest for Hugh Hefner. He gets the perfect GF who's there but not really there, and his every wish is her command. It's a boyfriend fantasy gone wild. But the show was every bit as popular with women, who understood that even though Major Nelson seemed to command Jeannie, in reality she was the one who pulled all the strings. No one could take her place, and nobody could outsmart her. Jeannie held the power because she was magic and because she was adored—by her fella, by his friends, and by millions of viewers across the country. Everyone could sign up for this home sweet home.

Each episode was a study in how Major Cutie and his magic GF worked through their issues. And they had a good setup. Jeannie would hang around the major's house all day, but she would return each night to her bottle, so he never had to worry about coming home to a house that had been redecorated or a bathroom overrun with makeup and hair products. Major Cutie's home remained his castle. They had come up with a not-quite-living-together arrangement that worked for them. And every couple knows how tricky that can be. But unless your life has been scripted by NBC, you need to be aware of the ground rules that will help make things go smoothly when you're on each other's turf.

## Quid Pro Quo

Once you are a couple, small, seemingly innocuous questions will start to come up. Can she leave her toothbrush at your place? Can she leave her underwear? What about her birth control? Are you going to give her a key? Don't fool yourself. The toothbrush means something—not as much as the key, but it all counts. Your GF will want to leave her stuff at your house. It makes her feel like she has a place there, that you're inviting her back.

Freak you out?

We understand if you don't want to go there. It is the first step toward cohabitation and away from an independent you. But you need to know that this is how your GF considers those panties in your bureau: You own something of hers and, quid pro quo, she owns a little bit of you. So, if you're going to let her leave her undies in your room among your old baseball hats and your collection of Sea Monkeys, don't pretend it doesn't mean anything.

The same rule applies to leaving stuff at her place. If she likes you at all, she'll like your stuff at her house. It means you feel at home there and, most important, that you'll be coming back. Unlike you, she probably won't be freaked out by this first step toward cohabitation; in fact, she'll find it exciting. Your girlfriend likes having your things around. They remind her of you. Your size-ten Nikes, Old Navy shirts, and huge jeans make her feel feminine because they are so masculine. And believe it or not, throwing your dirty T-shirts in the washing machine with her dirty T-shirts can be kind of a thrill. It's not that we love doing laundry; it's that it makes us feels connected to you and special. And by the way, we get this feeling doing a lot of things for you—not just domestic-goddess chores.

## GPS—*Girlfriend Positioning System*

**Guys like the house cold. Girls like it warm. Keep the thermostat up, and you'll have a better chance of seeing her naked.**

## *Key Notes*

To key or not to key, that is the question. Giving your GF a key, or letting her give you one, is a major step up from leaving your 501s on her bedpost. If you give her a key, the upside can be tremendous. You arrive home from work and there she is, waiting for you . . . naked. Conversely, you can leave little notes or presents for her, or be there with dinner waiting . . . naked. Inviting, isn't it? Of course, there is a downside. If you break up and she goes psycho, she can sneak into your pad, expose your film, steal the pants to all your suits, and—unbeknownst to you—use your toothbrush as a rectal thermometer. (True story.)

Asking for the key back can get ugly. We have a pal who moved on from GF #1 to GF #2, and although he had officially broken up with his old girlfriend, he couldn't face asking for his key back. In the middle of the night, GF #1 showed up in his bedroom where GF #2 was sleeping blissfully in his arms. It wasn't pretty. GF #1 wanted to kill GF #2 and then rip her head off and eat it. Think Godzilla vs. Mothra in Victoria's Secret. All this guy did wrong was offer up his key a little too easily. That's all. So remember, a key is heavy; don't go giving them away like breath mints.

Here are some key criteria. Ignore them at your own risk.

1. She has to be the only woman you are sleeping with— really and truly.

2. You have to be comfortable with the idea that she may show up to surprise you when you might not be in the mood to be surprised.

3. You have to like the idea that she might hang out at your house when you aren't home. (Is it okay if she looks through your drawers and those boxes in the closet? Because she probably will.)

4. You have to be okay with the notion that she might answer your phone.

5. You have to be okay with her knowing some of your secrets.

If you screw up and find you've given your key to a total nut job, you can always have the locks changed while she's at work.

## BE PREPARED

Your GF will always want more pillows on the bed and on the couch. Any flat surface where people might perch, she will want to "pillowize." Guys don't get pillows. From your point of view, the couch is already soft. Besides, when you sit down, you usually throw the pillows on the floor. Same with the bed. Fellas, the term is "pillow creep." Much like mold or fungus, it's hard to kill. It's possible to contain, but be prepared: It takes constant vigilance and effort. We know one BF who was driven to throwing them out the window to make his point. His GF came home and saw the lawn looking ripe for a 1960s love-in, and she finally got the message.

## *Feathering Your Nest*

Once your GF is comfortable at your house, or if she is really confident (read: "pushy"), she may have the urge to throw out your favorite plaid comforter and take over the decorating of your abode. Don't be intimidated. You can put your foot down.

> *Having a vagina doesn't mean she has cornered the market on taste. You are allowed to stick up for your orange shag carpeting.*

On the other hand, you could go with the flow and make the situation work for you. If your girlfriend has a passion for redecorating that borders on the obsessive-compulsive, there's every chance that she'll take the time to find the perfect couch, table, towel, or Grillmaster (see: shopping gene). Think of it as trading up. She will slyly chuck your 50 percent polyester sheets and bring in something 100 percent cotton with at least a 200 thread count (no need for you to understand that). She will replace your old gym socks on the coffee table with scented candles, which you can't wear to a basketball game but will smell a whole lot better. She will probably bring over or buy you a few new towels, because although yours are only four months old, you have never washed them, and they smell like mildew and the lint comes off on her body when she dries herself. She might even throw a lovely rug over that stain on the carpet, the one that has been there since your last GF threw a bowl of clam chowder at your head. This kind of attention doesn't suck, and let's face it, unless they have cats, girls' apartments usually smell a whole lot better than boys'.

## *American Standard*

A word about the toilet seat. There's a school of thought that believes the position of the toilet seat to be the man's exclusive responsibility. We beg to differ.

Sure, at your GF's place, the toilet seat should stay down. We sit down. It stays down. Simple. So when you're at your GF's, please put the toilet seat back down after you pee, particularly at night. (There's nothing worse for us girls than unexpectedly dunking our lalas in cold toilet water at three A.M.) You do that, and when we're at your place, we'll give you the home-court advantage. You like it up? We can oblige. It will be our turn to put the seat up after we're finished, no questions asked.

Our research has uncovered that many boyfriends have toilet-paper issues. Often there is none in the house for weeks at a time. We hate to think how you manage without it. You must purchase TP if you want us to continue to come over. It would also be great if you could actually put it on the TP holder, but we'll take what we can get. Also, please don't buy the cheapest brand, because we aren't that psyched about wiping our hoo-haas with something that feels like a page from *The New York Times*.

One last thing. Can we please discuss that après pee shaking? We don't know if this is a primal marking-your-territory sort of thing, but little drops all over the bathroom are disgusting. Same goes for those unexpected sticky spots on the floor. So be considerate: Shake with discretion.

## Be It Ever So Humble

You and your GF may not share the same idea of clean and tidy. That's okay. We're here not to convert you but to enlighten you. We are not saying you should roll over and play dead while she turns your fortress into an advertisement for *Elle Decor*, but she'll be much happier hanging out at your place if it meets her minimal requirements of clean. If she starts covering your newly purchased toilet paper (see, you listened!) with crocheted cozies, wants you to get a Hello Kitty bath mat, or starts talking about "accent" colors, put your foot down. But if you let

> Bottom line: A man's home is his castle, but if your castle is gross, we are not coming over. If getting naked in grubby surroundings is a continual test of our lust for you, eventually, we are going to fail.

her trade in your nasty taupe sheets for some lovely Wamsuttas (they can even be in a manly tone), she just might want to lie around in bed all day.

We know you guys are worried that we always want to change you. And we do. But if you want to have a GF, you've got to find a compromise between living like a college freshman and being taken over by the ghost of Martha. We are asking you to consider your GF's comfort, and our suggestions are eminently practical. That means: Buy real toilet paper instead of swiping the napkins from the pizza joint down the street. Make sure you have real shampoo in the bathroom, not some diluted Palmolive dish soap. If your dust bunnies are the size of real bunnies, buy a vacuum. Clean up a little, get the bare necessities like some low-fat milk for her coffee (to show you noticed), and you've just proved yourself worth the price of admission.

# CHAPTER 10

# WE INTERRUPT THIS PROGRAM...

## *Our friend Buck uses pro wrestling as a way* to avoid his girlfriend. Apparently, watching fat men dressed as Zorro jump on each other is the only way he can get a little peace and quiet. Becoming single or trading up seems like a better solution. But to each his own.

The television, like the Swiss Army knife, can be used for a broad range of functions. It can be a way to relax together or gently avoid each other, a shared escape, or an excuse to snuggle in the dark. It can be an education, a laugh riot, and foreplay, all without leaving your couch. In Buck's case, it can be girlfriend-resistant to 900 feet. Watching the whole first season of *The Shield* on DVD, eating takeout, and having an intermission for sex is a great way to spend a rainy Sunday. It might even beat out a cozy fire.

Women consider watching TV to be couples time, while men think of it as low-impact intimacy, a way to be together without having to fully engage. Your GF can be captivated while watching *Lost*, immersed in her feelings and loving it, and you can enjoy emoting (yes, that really is a word), too, because the drama is at a safe distance (some deserted island) and TV is a spectator sport. She thinks you're sharing a deeply moving experience; you think you're sharing a great story, and those tears in your eyes are only scoring you points. Never have you paid so little to get so much.

## Remote Possibilities

The suffragette movement gave women the vote, but it couldn't foresee the remote. To get the remote into neutral territory would take a picket line, a strike, or another showdown like the Alamo. You guys act like the remote is some kind of sacred instrument, as if it requires the artistry, skill, and intuition necessary to pilot the *Millennium Falcon*. Women, it seems, are simply not qualified to handle this hallowed device. We have a friend, Mark, who brings the remote with him to the bathroom so his GF won't usurp his authority. He has even confessed to taking the batteries out of the damn thing when he's gone, in order to protect his domain. Just because it's shaped like a penis doesn't make it your birthright. There is something called the Equal Rights Amendment (yeah, we know it's never been ratified, but you still have to pay attention to it if you want to keep a GF). How about this: We'll concede primary management of the remote, but you have to ceremoniously share it a few times a year, and you must consider that women watch TV differently than you do. Yes, we're talking about FVPs—feminine viewing patterns.

As you watch TV together, you will learn (yet again) that your girlfriend is constructed differently than you are. She's not going to channel-surf, and you're probably not going to stop. She'll settle in with whatever looks best, and it probably won't have "ultimate fighting" or "monster truck" in the title. So do the right thing. Mix it up. What harm could it possibly do you to sit through a Lifetime movie every once in a while? And even if the "women in crisis" flick she forces you to watch makes you cry, remember crying releases testosterone, which deepens your voice. In the long run, the whole experience may even make you manlier.

## What Did I Miss?

Women like to talk. Everywhere. Home, work, the library, the ladies' room, the gym, the produce department, the Department of Motor Vehicles, the Department of Revenue, and the lingerie department at Macy's. But it doesn't end

## GIRL ON GIRL
### Advice for Your Girlfriend!

When the television goes on, guys go into a meditative state; it's impenetrable. Here's why: Guys do one thing at a time. When they make love, they make love. They don't think about work, having dinner, or whether they picked up the mail, the way we might. Let him watch the show uninterrupted, and if you really, really need his attention, turn off the TV or take off your clothes or both.

there. We like to talk when we're watching television, too. Obviously, if there's talking, there's not much watching going on. We get that. It's just that the silence required for serious TV viewing sometimes causes in us an uncontrollable impulse to check in with you. Nothing serious, simply idle chatter. We don't consider it truly disruptive; however, it probably gets in the way of your enjoyment. You guys like to tune in, zone out, and watch. We like to participate. Look at the success of Home Shopping Network. So don't let our need to chat ruin what could otherwise be a perfect moment. Spell it out for us. Give us the small print like they do in the Prilosec commercial. Stake out your territory and tell us which shows are no-jabber zones. If we don't respect your request, there is always duct tape.

## BE PREPARED

Ever notice that when you sit down to watch TV, your GF plops her feet in your lap without saying a word? It's not a favor, not a trade-off, not a request. In fact, there's no question about it: She wants you to rub her feet. This comes from the part of us that resembles cats. They jump in your lap, you rub. Don't ruin it by making her rub your feet in return. We consider this fair, since you hog the remote.

## *TV Guide*

Sure, you and your GF both want to watch *American Idol*, *The Office*, and *Grey's Anatomy*, but you'd sit through a twelve-hour marathon of *This Old House*, *American Chopper*, or *Star Trek*, and she'd spend her Memorial Day weekend watching every period film Colin Firth has ever made. Just remember the rules: Share and share alike. Everyone gets a turn.

The good news is, if you sit down with your GF and watch something girly like *Sex and the City*, you'll see a lot of nubile young tatas, sexual oddities, and maybe some girl-on-girl action. So don't be so quick to protest. You may find you like this variety in your diet.

# CHAPTER 11

# JUST WHAT I'VE ALWAYS WANTED

***In the busy life of a boyfriend, the subject of presents*** might not be considered a priority, and compared with some other aspects of your relationship, they are a minor point. But we're giving the subject its very own chapter because, as you may be noticing, things that may seem unimportant to you can be of profound significance to your girlfriend.

It's not that your GF has some rapacious need for gifts—consider cutting her loose if she does—it's that she looks at the timing and selection of the presents and sees an expression of your feelings. (Sound familiar? The thing you do isn't only the thing you do; it often represents something else.) That's why you need to think of the presents you give her as messages; as potent symbols, in fact. (And what boyfriend wants to be impotent?) A poorly chosen gift—a spatula, stapler, Costco membership—can send a poor message; whereas a well-chosen gift—her favorite perfume, a leather jacket, a trowel—can instantly transform you into a thoughtful romantic leading man.

## *You Shouldn't Have*

We know the question of gifts can be intimidating, but there are rules, and if you know them, you can approach the selection process with confidence. Don't just blow it off with "I don't know what to get her" or "She's too hard to shop for." As they say in preschool, put on your "listening ears," because if you do, you will soon realize that in any given week, your GF will mention in passing seventeen things that she wants. At least. So take note. She walks by a store window and lusts after a shirt; she compliments a handbag someone else is holding; she mentions she's out of her favorite perfume, spaghetti sauce, or sports socks. Make lists if you have to, or wear a wire so you can review the conversation later, when you are alone. It really isn't as difficult as it seems. When you listen, you will start to learn her likes and dislikes, and that will make it easier to get her a gift she'll appreciate.

For that perfect present, go to chick stores, not hardware stores. Jewelry is always a big winner, but forget the friendship or commitment rings. The first time she should open

## *BE PREPARED*

**If listening isn't your strong suit, fake it. Get cashmere.**

that little ring box is when you're asking her to marry you. Clothes are always a good idea, and if she doesn't like what you got her, you've given her a legitimate reason to go shopping to exchange it. Feel free to ask her girlfriends; they will know what she likes. Shoes, too, are always welcome. They may seem like a very specific, personal, and somewhat utilitarian present, but to your GF they are a never-ending source of joy. Just check in her closet for her size and favorite designer.

Need some other ideas? A sexy anytime present can be something you already own: your faded, soft college T-shirt that she loves (and will wear around the house with nothing else on), your baseball hat, or a picture of you when you were a kid. She will love a gift that reminds her of you. In general, we don't suggest giving home appliances: blenders, Dust-Busters, toasters, bowls, etc. And we certainly don't recommend a ThighMaster. As much as she may need these items, what they lack in the romance department far outweighs the useful factor. On the other hand, if your GF is a real foodie and loves to cook and bake, then you can score with a cool appliance. A KitchenAid mixer she's always wanted in a funky color, or a cappuccino maker for two, would make a great gift. And while we're on the subject of appliances, a sex toy or vibrator might really hit the spot. If sex toys are already a part of your repertoire, go ahead and get her the rotating vibrator with the buzzing gerbil on top. But remember: This toy, like a cordless drill, is really for you, so you better throw in a box of chocolates.

## *One Size Doesn't Fit All*

How are you supposed to come up with the right present for *your* GF? Remember, the best choice is not necessarily the most expensive. If you listen to women swooning over the presents they love (and they will), you'll find that they're more impressed by the creativity and thoughtfulness than they are by price. The key to success is getting your GF a gift that reflects her personality, one that says, "I know who you are and what you like, and most of all, I have been listening."

- **What are her dreams?** Does she have a secret fantasy of being a rock star? Get her a guitar (secondhand stores are a great resource) and some really cool black underwear to wear with it.

- **Does she like to read?** Oprah's Book Club always has great picks, so if your GF is an avid reader, you could start there. If you have an idea of other books she's enjoyed, your local bookstore staff should be able to help you choose something based on those. Or you could get her a subscription to her favorite magazine, say *American Banker* or *Welding for Women.*

- **Does she like flowers?** Is there one that will remind her of your early dates? Does she love lilacs? Does she like a flower that fills the house with fragrance, such as tuberose, or would she prefer an herb garden for the windowsill?

- **Does she love to laugh?** Here are some ideas: Wrap up the first season of *Seinfeld*, the latest from David Sedaris, or perform your own interpretation of *Swan Lake*—tutu optional.

- **Does she love to pamper herself?** You can't go wrong with a gift certificate to her favorite spa for a facial, manicure, or pedicure. When you send her away to indulge herself on your dime, you have just become the ultimate sugar daddy.

- **Does she love great leather?** Not that kind! Get her a gorgeous change purse or wallet.

- **Does she love a label?** While it's true that Prada and Gucci are out of most people's price range, there are affordable alternatives. Isaac Mizrahi at Target has great goodies. In some circles, Fruit of the Loom is considered a label.

- **Mementos are great.** Have you been together for a while? We know a guy who scored by giving his GF the matchbook in which she originally wrote her number, nestled in a tiny silver box.

Follow this advice and you can avoid that last-minute run to the lingerie store where your palms are sweating and the shopgirl looks at you with pity. If, however, that last-minute trip is necessary, a word about sizing: Go small on the panties and big on the bra. None of it will fit, but she'll think that's how you remember her: small butt, big boobs. Points? Say no more.

## Out of the Blue

Don't wait for holidays or birthdays. The out-of-nowhere, just-because-I'm-into-you gift will take her breath away and may even provide you with a fistful of invisible "Get Out of Jail Free" cards. Give her a gift to say "I'm thinking about you" or "You snore." Again, we're not talking about spending money. It's not the alumni campaign, the PBS pledge drive, or organ donation—unless you're lucky. These gifts can be tiny and silly. Wrap up a pack of gum, a fridge magnet, a cupcake, an egg timer, or the latest copy of *Travel + Leisure*, the one with the cover story about the island she wants to visit. Just about anything from Walgreens will do: Barbie barrettes, a skateboard, bright pink bubble bath, a hula hoop, or Scooby Doo Band-Aids.

### Be creative. Coin your own holidays:

- Thank God We're Not Cousins or This Would Be Incest Day

- Because You Like Watching Dumb TV Day

- Thrilled You Like Hanging Out at My Place Day

- Potato Chips and Beer Day

- Because You Don't Mind Putting Up with Grouchy Me Day

- Official Stay in Bed All Day Day

- Happy You Look Good in a Little Black Dress Because I Don't Day

## Clear and Present Danger: The "Don't Even Think About It" Presents

**Compilation CDs.** These are not a sexy gift. In fact, they suck. You may have spent four hours putting together your favorite cuts of Death Cab for Cutie, All-American Rejects, Radio Head, Social Distortion, and Aerosmith, but your GF will not appreciate it. Do not, under any circumstances, give this as a Valentine's Day present.

**Regifting.** Your mother sent you coffee mugs with "CAF-FEINATED!" written on the side and a mohair scarf in alternating shades of brown and blue. Your office gave out free notepads with PROZAC printed on them. You have a bright green XXL T-shirt that says BIOPHEX PHARMACEUTICAL CONFERENCE 1998. Two words: "Goodwill Industries." We GFs have a great nose for sniffing out hand-me-down presents, so take note: In many languages, "regifting" means "ex-boyfriend."

**Plastic surgery.** If you have the bucks for this, spend it on a trip to Aruba and love her nose, ass, boobs, or whatever the way the good Lord made them.

**Anything that belonged to your ex.** We have a friend who gave his GF a shirt that his ex had given him. It was a really cool vintage shirt—quite a find. But it landed him in the doghouse, and the shirt found its way into the paper shredder. (This rule also applies to anything you bought for your ex but never got around to giving her. We can usually sniff that out, too.)

**Gift certificates to hardware stores.** This is the present she should give you. It proves that old saying "just get her something you would like" to be bullshit.

**Weight Watchers or Jenny Craig membership.** If you are signing her up for this kind of program, you have signed up for the wrong girl. We have said it before, but it bears repeating: Love what's in front of you, or move on.

**Cash.** Not a good gift unless you're dating a hooker. On the other hand, if it's five grand or more, we want it.

## Welcome to the Doghouse

The "I'm sorry" gift takes a little more thought. If you really have been a bad boy, then it's easy. Max out your Visa, and back the delivery truck up to her house. But what if she's mad at you and it's not your fault? Maybe it's a misunderstanding. Your instinct might be not to give a present at this juncture. Why eat humble pie when it's not what you ordered and not what you deserve? Pay attention now, this is A-game stuff. There are presents that say "Let's drop it and make up." How about flowers? Yes, the suggestion is obvious and simple, but they work. Flowers with a short note are a cure-all for the common clash. It's not a sweater, which works for birthdays or Christmas; nor is it apology jewelry, which is an absolute admission of guilt. It's a gesture, and yes, in this case it *is* the thought that counts.

And then there's the present that *puts* you in the doghouse. Our friend Kate just told us the story of her twenty-eighth birthday. Her boyfriend, Rob, bought her two days at a great spa. She was dreaming of sugar scrubs, scented massage oil, and mud baths that would leave her ten pounds lighter and ten clicks hotter on the sexy scale. Perfect, right? Except that on her actual birthday, which was a Saturday, her boyfriend opted to go to work instead of spending the day with her. Bad move. It wrecked the birthday present and soured all his hard work. While she could have been relaxing under the hands of Svetlana, the tsarina of rejuvenation, she was feeling abandoned and lonely because Rob would rather spend her birthday at work than with her.

Our advice: Skip the spa, take the day off, and be with her. Have some fun. Stay in bed and watch TV. Go for a hike. Make her breakfast. Put her underwear on your head and dance to the theme music from *Star Wars*. It's not about

# It's the Thought That Counts . . .
# Unless It's a Crappy Thought

Our friend Brenda e-mailed her colleagues for bad-gift stories. Her mailbox was overcapacity within five minutes:

- "The jerk gave me a silver cuff bracelet in a Tiffany's box. It was my first gift from Tiffany's, and I was thrilled to open that beautiful blue box. Years later, I found out the darn thing was worth nothing and not from Tiffany's at all. My hint? My wrist turned green."

- "I got a pair of boob-shaped candles. Who did he think he was dating, Howard Stern?"

- "George tries so hard, but he never really gets it right. This year, for my birthday, he got me a pair of enormous Juicy Couture dangly rhinestone earrings, in spite of the fact that A) I never wear jewelry and B) I am not Beyoncé. Also: Juicy Couture makes earrings?"

- "Nothing is as bad as my dad. My mom would really love some fancy costume jewelry, but in the past three years, she has received:
    - a set of golf clubs
    - golf lessons
    - a model boat (the last one made me seriously worried that divorce was imminent)."

- "A basket of bath products from Filene's Basement, in a citrus scent, which is one of my least favorite flavors or smells in the entire world. This was in our *third* year together."

- "I had been going out with a guy for a year, and he gave me an envelope of money with the explanation 'I didn't know what to get you.'"

- "You won't believe this, but for our anniversary, he gave me a cell phone he got for free when he purchased his own. For our first Christmas, he got me fly-fishing gear that he later 'borrowed' back. This was a theme: books he'd wanted to read, stationery he needed, some stereo that he found exciting. (I still use my eighth-grade boom box.) For our last Christmas together, he gave me cooking classes (he went halfsies with his mom). Actually, I completely enjoyed the classes, and now I make yummy dinners with my new boyfriend, John."

- "A Fighting Irish finger puppet. Yes, you heard right."

the value of the gift. It's about making a gesture that says you value her.

And if you really want to make us love you, think of what we call rainy-day gifts. Cool old-fashioned bookends, picture frames, anything you might find in a flea market, coffee-table books, vases, little embroidered couch pillows, soft throw blankets: These all have the cozy factor. All that's missing is a rainy day and you.

## Wrapping It Up

You may consider yourself God's gift to women, but we still want presents. Here's why: We girls talk to show our feelings (over and over and over). It is how we connect, how we show we care, how we share ourselves with those we love. You guys don't communicate in the same way, but we're good at adapting. We remind ourselves you can't get water from a stone or long-winded answers from the average heterosexual male. As a result, we look for the input from you in other ways. That's why it's not about the price tag of the gift; it's about the priceless quality of your attention and connection.

# CHAPTER 12

# CLOTHES MAKE THE MAN

***There are a lot of things we're un-
sure of in this world:*** Does a stitch in time
actually save nine? Are you *really* what you eat? And if a
penny saved is in fact a penny earned, do we need to list it on
our tax return? We prefer to leave these and other imponder-
ables to the experts (like the dry cleaner, the dietician, and
the accountant), but one thing we know is true: Clothes
make the man.

Your choice of garment tells the world who you are. From
your GF's point of view, it tells the world who she's sleeping
with, so you can be sure she's going to care how you turn yourself out. Some of you guys are naturally stylish, and she can
follow your lead. But others have a garment test that goes like
this: Is it clean? Does it fit? Is it all in one piece? If the answer
is yes to two out of three, you're good to go. But here comes
your GF, hinting, helping, and sometimes harping. It's always
nice to get tips from an expert, but it can get to the point
where you feel like a BF mannequin, and who wants that?

It's not about trying to impress your GF by spending a
month's rent on a pair of shoes; nor is it about becoming a
metrosexual. We don't care whether you're a hedge-fund
manager or a geography teacher. We are here to offer guid-

ance so your clothes don't detract from your charm and good looks, and which will save you from feeling like you are being pushed around by your GF. You may think we care about what kind of car you drive or the size of your, ahem, big-screen TV, and we won't lie to you, we do. But we're really interested in a man who's comfortable in his own skin, who knows how to match his socks to each other and doesn't ask, "Smell these—are they clean?"

> Clothes may express your inner man, but if he could see you in that corduroy suit, he might want a different representative.

## Bare Necessities

In the same way you wouldn't get her a fabulous piece of jewelry and wrap it in a paper bag, you don't want to be going around in some sad underwear that doesn't show the family jewels to their advantage. Young John and the twins deserve better.

Underwear really is important. Like Superman and his X-ray vision, girls have a supernatural ability, especially when it comes to men's underwear. In a crowded room, we can pick out which guy is wearing cool boxers or totally lame briefs. Briefs—what we call "man-panties"—are disgusting, and you shouldn't wear them. Girls like boxers. We think they're sexy, that they leave something to the imagination.

What's more, they don't give us the outline of your package, all squished up and scary, like strange sea creatures. Trust us: We don't want to see what you would look like in a Speedo every time you take off your pants. And another thing: Boxers hold up better over time. A ratty old pair of briefs, all gray and stained and full of holes, makes a man look like he belongs in an orphanage.

If you like the support that briefs afford and don't want all your dangling bits dangling around, there are some cool, flattering compromises out there:

- **2(x)ist** may carry a somewhat higher price tag, but, like the perfect pair of black pants, 2(x)ist make every body and butt look good.

- **T-box** performs the same task as a magnifying glass. The front acts like a kind of codpiece to make even the most challenged package look huge. If you've ever seen a Shakespeare play, you know how flattering a codpiece can be to those Two Gentlemen of Verona.

- **Stanfields** are a sexy variation on the Wild Wild West long underwear you see on the old reruns of *Gunsmoke*. They have two buttons (purely ornamental) and make a guy look rugged and tough.

- **Banana Republic** boxers aren't as form-fitting as T-box or 2(x)ist; they're more along the lines of the classic boxer. They give you room to swing without leaving you twisting in the wind.

We're traditionalists, though, and believe that the classic boxer is the way to go. If you need more convincing, check out any of those Abercrombie & Fitch ads. Sure, the pictures are geared to the *Brokeback Mountain* crowd, but you can't deny how fantastic the underwear looks. They fade in a cool sexy way—think Ivy League, summers sailing in Maine, making coffee in the morning with your GF and a yellow Lab at your side. Or if you live on the West Coast, think surfers, who wouldn't be caught dead in briefs. And if you need any further persuasion, know that the sight of a grown man in a pair of tighty whities pulled up over his belly button makes us want to smash your head in.

## The Jean Pool and Other Considerations

It doesn't get much sexier than a guy in the right pair of jeans and a T-shirt. As American as apple pie, favored by cowboys and made famous by movie stars, jeans have become a way of life, a fashion statement, a fashion staple, and a money pit. Even the Dalai Lama wears jeans, but only when he's in

## BE PREPARED

Boxers are more forgiving than briefs. Love handles don't seep down over the sides, and they make your legs and waist look good—no ifs, ands, or butts.

Aspen visiting Goldie Hawn. The kind of jeans you wear—and how you wear them—speak volumes not just about your ass but about you. Jeans can turn your GF on or make her gag. As your most low-maintenance, ready-for-anything look, jeans are probably your first choice. You throw them on and you're done. But not so fast, mister . . . we need to discuss a little thing called fit.

**America's crack problem.** Trends come and go—and come and go, and come and go—but here's a good rule of thumb: If your jeans are resting right on top of your crotch, they are too low. We don't want to see your pubic hair, and we really don't want to see Crackatowa. Also, what is the point of reaching for your wallet down by your knees and having yards and yards of fabric pooling around your kicks?

**Mom jeans.** If you haven't gone out to buy jeans in eight years, you are wearing "mom" jeans. We guarantee they are too tight, too loose, too high-waisted, pleated, or too short. Seeing a guy in mom jeans can permanently extinguish the flames of desire. Let your mom wear mom jeans, and go get yourself a couple of new pairs every year.

**These guns for hire.** Cutting off the sleeves of your button-down shirt to highlight your guns only flies if you're one of the Dukes of Hazzard. If you need to show off your arms (which we applaud), a formfitting white T-shirt rocks.

**Seepage.** Avoid clothes that are too tight. If you've put on a few pounds, get yourself a bigger pair of jeans. And be aware that all parts of the body expand when you put on weight, not just the part that your jeans cover. We know a guy who got too fat for his glasses. If your shirt is feeling a bit tight around your neck, pay attention. We can forgive the weight gain, but it's impossible to have a conversation with a guy who looks like his blood flow is being slowly cut off by his collar.

**Suit yourself.** Suits are sexy; invest in a good one. We mean it, although we're not sure you guys believe us. The sight of a man in a well-tailored suit can make a girl's heart skip a beat. We don't care about ties, per se, just don't wear ones with race cars or golfers on them.

**A shoe-in.** Bad shoes are a neon light blinking RUN AWAY to potential girlfriends. You can go to a lot of trouble with your ensemble, and if your shoes are geeky, disgusting, or look like they were made in Eastern Europe, all your work has gone to waste. We don't need a fashion plate. Philip Seymour Hoffman is adorable in his scruffiosity, but even he (who believes that a sweatshirt the cat has been sleeping on is haute couture) always has cool shoes. If your idea of high style is a pair of Danskin character shoes (standard choice for mimes), get a new idea.

**A note on knit caps.** We know they were cool last year or maybe even last week, but even in their day, you looked really stupid in them. Guys thought they looked like Ashton Kutcher, Brad Pitt, or Colin Farrell, and really they looked like reservoir-tipped condoms. Come on, even Jack Nicholson turned the edge up, turning the look into a "studley watch cap" instead of "refugee from a Dr. Seuss book."

*Someone once described sweatpants as the death of hope, and we agree. Wear them only when you want to inspire existential despair, thereby making yourself less desirable.*

**He died with his boots on.** Unless you live in Texas, do not wear cowboy boots (or cowboy hats) with a suit. This was acceptable in the 1980s when *Dallas* was the hottest show on TV, but unless your day job involves roping and branding, steer clear.

## A Clothes Call
## What You See/What She Sees

*YOU SEE:* Your tank top made from that cool mesh material with the NASCAR logo. Sexy and pleasantly cool.

*SHE SEES:* A window not into your soul but into the bushy thatch of your underarm hair. Confirmation that only Bubba and Olympic skaters should wear mesh anything.

*YOU SEE:* That Guatemalan vest you got when you went down to South America to build houses with Habitat for

Humanity. You're a world traveler, socially conscious, wearing a hip blue vest that really complements your eyes.

**SHE SEES:** A refugee from the 70s and a vest that should have been canceled along with *The Sonny and Cher Show*.

**YOU SEE:** A buff guy in a sexy gym outfit that shows all your best qualities. Perfect for picking up girls.

**SHE SEES:** Herman the German poking out of his too-short shorts. Proof that spandex should be outlawed.

**YOU SEE:** Your hilarious T-shirt with FUCK YOGA on the front.

**SHE SEES:** Your hilarious T-shirt with FUCK YOGA on the front.

## And So to Bed

What to wear to bed? If you're with your girlfriend, she'll usually want you to wear your birthday suit. Some guys don't feel comfortable sleeping in their altogether and will pull on a pair of their cool underwear (detailed above) and a T-shirt. Fine, so long as you draw the line at matching flannel PJs. Your girlfriend wants to sleep with her BF, not her little brother. If you can pull off a pair of those cool loose pants, worn without a shirt over your morning cup of coffee, your GF will want to pull you back to bed. Just know that whatever you wear or don't wear to bed, you need to avoid earplugs, eye masks, snore guards, socks, the same shirt you worked out in, and silk pajamas—unless

# *Natty Dressers Throughout History*

**LOUIS XIV:** Wore wigs and high heels, but the ladies still lined up. It's good to be Sun King.

**TEDDY ROOSEVELT:** A man's man, the leader of the free world. Built like a squat lineman but managed to be a snappy dresser whether in suits or safari gear. Made John Lennon glasses the rage long before the British Invasion.

**ALBERT EINSTEIN:** The guy had ten girlfriends, and if you can wear a porkpie hat, a rumpled suit, and still come up with the theory of relativity, whatever you do is fashion.

**JAMES BOND:** So he's fictional; from Connery to Craig, the way Bond wears a simple black tux makes him truly licensed to kill.

**LONE RANGER:** He made tight white pants, gloves with fringe, and black masks mysterious and sexy. If you can make a horse come when you call, you're doing something right.

**BARACK OBAMA:** The New Statesman, sleek and graceful. Conservative dark suits with understated ties. If handsome is as handsome does, this guy is a winner on both fronts.

**DAVID LETTERMAN:** It's hard to notice anything beyond the gap in his teeth and his rapier wit, but as he buttons and unbuttons his jacket and continually strokes his tie, we are reminded of the phrase "too sexy for his shirt." We wonder what it would be like to be unbuttoned and stroked by him.

**JOLLY GREEN GIANT:** Knew how to work with his height and stuck to solid colors, which are slimming.

**WINNIE-THE-POOH:** Love his warm and cuddly look, although we're on the fence about his decision to go without pants.

you are Al Pacino in *Scarface*, an elderly invalid, or an editor from *Hustler* magazine.

## *Employees Must Wash Hands Before Returning to Work*

Now that we have covered most of the things that go on top of your beautiful self, what about your beautiful self itself? What about those nose hairs, for example? You may think they're the sole property of Grandpa Clark, but believe us, the tragedy of unruly nose hairs can happen to anyone at any time. And as with most devastating tragedies, those who are closest to you are hit the hardest. It is impossible for your girlfriend to listen to what you are saying, or give you some good loving, when all she sees are those nose hairs screaming out of your nostrils like teenage girls reaching for a rock star. If you take care of those pesky nose hairs, bats in the cave won't be a problem, either. We beg you, get a nose-hair trimmer and use it. The same goes for your ears and the top of your nose. (Actually, most girlfriends like this part of the grooming process and would be happy to help; it appeals to us in the same way that popping blackheads on your back does. Oh, don't say, "Gross.") And speaking of blackheads, every so often check out your skin close up. Some of you guys have blackheads that are older than your GF. Or maybe that's where they buried Jimmy Hoffa.

Dirty fingernails are okay if you have just come in from work, but on a night out, they just look grubby. On the other hand (no pun intended), unless you are a character from *The Sopranos* or a hand model (what?), you shouldn't get your fingernails buffed or, God forbid, lacquered. That's our department, and we don't like to share. Waxed or plucked eyebrows scare us, too. You may think it makes you look less like a caveman, but actually, you look more like a transvestite or a Japanese character actress. Of course, it is advisable to trim your eyebrows, especially when they're so long as to be suitable for braiding. Just know when to stop.

With regard to cologne, less really is more. Don't wear so much that it clings to our skin after a kiss or snuggle. It makes us feel like we are going out with our Uncle Morty. The truth

You're never fully dressed without a smile, so how's yours? It usually takes a young nephew or niece to point out how yellow or gray your teeth are. But don't kid yourself. They're just saying what's been on everyone's mind. Pay attention to your teeth and your breath will improve, and so will your chances of playing a few games of tonsil hockey. We'd even go so far as to recommend teeth whitening. You can get those whitening strips at the drugstore, and they make a huge difference. While you're there, pick up some mints, because if you don't have sweet breath, then you have the other kind: coffin breath, death breath, morning breath, bar breath, coffee breath . . . The list goes on. It will be hard for your girlfriend to mention because she doesn't want to hurt your feelings, but God invented Altoids for a reason.

is, we love the way you smell—most of the time. However, sometimes ripe gets too ripe. We don't love your smell mixed with traffic, a workout that happened two hours ago, stale air, and stress. That we classify as "flop sweat," and it's bad.

And while we're on the subject, we know it's hard to remember to check yourself, but earwax is sneaky and disgusting. Invest in some Q-tips, and add them to your daily regimen, because whispering sweet nothings into yellow goo takes the fun out of it. Watch out for eye boogers, too. These happen to everyone, but we want to see your baby blues or browns without the crumbs.

We realize that our call to arms is not going to cause a run on nose-hair clippers. Old habits die hard, and we acknowledge that there have been men throughout history with dirty nails and horrific body odor who have gone on to lead full and satisfying lives. But believe us, a little grooming in all the right places will make a big difference to your GF. It's not that cleanliness is next to godliness, it's that without cleanliness, you'll be sleeping alone.

> The message you think you are sending with your cool attire may look different from a female's perspective; one person's roast beef sandwich is another person's pile of bloody animal muscles between two pieces of gluten. In general, we vote for the classic over the trendy every time. Simplicity exudes confidence, so keep it simple. We like nothing better than a guy who isn't fussy and, no matter what he is wearing, will sit on the curb talking with his girl.

## Off the Cuff

This may sound sexist, but if your GF says, "You can't wear that," she's probably right. On the other hand, if you give her an inch, she'll take your whole wardrobe. "Yeah," you think, "if I listened to my GF's advice, I would have a better haircut, nicer shirts, and cool shoes, and I would be a nicer-dressed, better-groomed eunuch." How much can you allow her to tailor your look before it feels like she's snipped off your balls? At what point does she cross the boundaries and the whole thing becomes emasculating? Only you can know. It is great to get some advice from your GF, but if you find yourself up in arms over a pair of orange slacks, it's not about the pants, it's about what's in the pants. Take her advice only as long as you can still look in the mirror and feel like yourself. Changing your wardrobe should not become an attempt to change you.

# CHAPTER 13

# ON THE TOWN

### *The first time Jenny knew a boy liked her was when* Steven Goldstein hit her in the head with a soccer ball in third grade. It hurt like hell, but inside, she was thrilled. Not only did Steven *like* her, he had practically announced it to the whole school. Throwing a ball that hard, and in front of everyone on the playground, was, for a boy of eight, the equivalent of Tom Cruise proclaiming his love while jumping up and down on Oprah's couch. As Jenny sat in the nurse's office holding her ice pack, she realized her life had just changed.

In middle school, the dynamic began to shift. When a boy liked Jenny, he'd call, and they'd talk on the phone for hours. And when Jenny liked a boy, she'd pass him a note through a girlfriend. Once, feeling extra bold, she passed a note to Bobby Mortley with boxes to check:

**"Do you like me?"**

☐ A lot.
☐ A little.
☐ Just medium.

When the note came back, Jenny's heart leaped. Bobby had checked the top box. Twice. She was on cloud nine . . . that is, until the next day in the cafeteria, when he completely ignored her. Then she was crushed.

High school came as a relief. No more hair pulling, no more bonks on the head, no more about-face. When a boy liked Jenny, he talked, he flirted, and sometimes he even asked her out on a date. There were movies, there was pizza, there was the requisite kissing and fumbling around the bases. Still, no matter how impassioned those fumblings got, when Jenny saw her young paramour in the hallway the next day, her backseat Valentino had been mysteriously transformed into a diffident boy-beast who frowned at her from behind a barely there moustache. Jenny learned early on that it's one thing for a BF to let on that he likes you and another thing altogether for him to back that up in public. Your girlfriend learned the same lesson, and that's why your public persona will be scrutinized—very carefully. Can you blame her?

## Stepping Out

When you're at home, it's easy to treat your GF like she's the only woman in the room—chances are, she is. But when you're out on the town, there's a lot competing for your attention: your best friend, your BlackBerry, the bartender, the amazing set of boobs that just walked in the door. The world is watching, and make no mistake about it, so is your girlfriend.

Actions speak louder than words, and to your GF, your actions in public are deafening. Whether you're at the coffee shop, the birthday party, or the DMV, your girlfriend will want you to be the same attentive BF who was sliding off her thong last night. It's consistency she's looking for, and courtesy. These are the things that count with your girlfriend. Break out your shining armor, and she'll be so turned on, she'll peel it off with a can opener. Reveal your wandering-eyed inner cad, and she'll be looking for her next date harder than you are.

Sound tricky? It doesn't have to be. Don't think of this as another behavioral minefield to navigate. Think of it as a way to score huge points while expending a minimum of effort. Let's face it. The bar is set pretty low. A tiny gesture made in public—holding a door, standing when she returns to the table—will resonate powerfully. Treat her well in a roomful of people, and watch her eyes come up triple jackpot.

## She's with Me

We've all seen that guy who dates a girl again and again but never quite seems like he's with her. He keeps his distance, rarely touches her (until they get home), and never, but never, refers to himself as her boyfriend. This is a misguided attempt to play both sides of the fence. Like a realtor leaving a FOR SALE sign on a house that's not on the market, it's tacky, it's dishonest, and it serves no purpose. Women aren't stupid. We know he's with her, so we see a guy who likes to keep his options open. The irony, of course, is that when we see a guy dote on his date, lavishing her with care and attention, we think, "The minute she blows it, I am all over that."

We have a friend who always walked three paces ahead of his GF, as if he were royalty and she was bringing up the rear. Finally, she got upset and pointed it out to him, but he didn't see why it was such a big deal. To him it was an old habit, one he was completely unaware of. But this habit spoke volumes to his GF. She felt his speed-walking was like a sign around his neck that read I'M NOT REALLY WITH HER. She, like many women, was extremely sensitive to those acts that spoke to her value. It's one of those neurotic traits that you will have to contend with, despite the fact that it may have been in place long before you came into the picture.

# BE PREPARED

Almost anything you do or say can be seen as a statement that expresses our relative value in the world and, more importantly, in your heart. We're not proud of this, but we know we're not alone in it. Don't forget: You have your own currency issues to deal with, and sometimes, when it comes to the self-esteem market, we give you a very favorable exchange rate.

# On the Town
# What He Sees/What She Sees

## The Office Christmas Party

*HE SEES:* A roomful of pals, free booze, and an opportunity to party with the boss.

*SHE SEES:* A roomful of people she doesn't know and a BF who can't wait to make his mark with Maker's Mark, while she's subjected to Ed from Accounting's thrilling monologue about his days as a Trekkie. Again.

## A Dinner Date

*HE SEES:* His GF arriving at the dinner party. He's glad to see her, but can't go over and give her a kiss, because he doesn't want to be rude to his friend, who's in the middle of a story.

*SHE SEES:* A BF who can't spare a moment from his conversation to welcome her. Guess she should have stayed home.

## A Romantic Evening

*HE SEES:* A guy who takes her out for an expensive dinner the same night as the big fight on HBO. What sacrifice, what consideration, what a lover. (So what if he checks the score once in a while?)

*SHE SEES:* A lonely girl forced to spend a disastrous evening with a crabby, distracted boyfriend who keeps checking his BlackBerry while rushing through dinner.

The good news is, it doesn't take much to make your girlfriend feel cared for. Our friend Sarah, at lunch with her BF, Reed, became worried that the slow service would make her late getting back to the office. Reed heard her concern and politely told the waiter that they were on a tight schedule. He handled it without her having to ask and impressed her with his consideration and his take-charge manner. These little considerations build up like frequent-flyer miles: When you accumulate enough, you can trade them in for a first-class ticket—into her pants. May sound simple, but that's how it works. When we feel loved, appreciated, and taken care of, we want you. Bad.

## Not Here

Most of the time, your GF will be more comfortable with public displays of affection—PDAs—than you are. Our pal Daniel once pleaded, "Why do I have to hold your hand and sit glued to you in the back of this spacious cab? Can't I just adore you with my eyes?" The answer, sadly, is no. Your GF's thirst for affection, public or private, can be almost unquenchable. Sure, you'll put your arm around her in the movies, hold hands here and there, and even kiss on the street once in a while, but in general, a big gulp for you is barely a sip to her.

What's the problem? Why is she intent on sharing your relationship with the world? Hard to say. Sometimes she'll do it out of love, sometimes out of insecurity, and sometimes because she likes showing off: "Look at the hot guy I'm with, and look how into me he is." If that's the case, it means your girlfriend thinks you're worth showing off, so consider yourself lucky. If it makes you uncomfortable, gently provide guidelines that will recognize her needs while expressing yours. Explain that snuggling in the checkout line at 7-Eleven makes you queasy, that your soft side is reserved for more private places such as the couch or the bedroom or the kitchen floor. The fact is, this is one of those areas where you will both have to live outside your comfort zone. You'll have to get mushy sometimes when you're not feeling it, and she'll have to live with wanting a little more than she'll get.

# *What to Do When You're Out on the Town*

**A CHEAT SHEET SUITABLE FOR FOLDING UP AND PUTTING IN YOUR WALLET**

- When you walk into a restaurant or a party and your girlfriend is already there, don't mingle. Even if you saw her an hour ago, make a bee-line for her and plant a big smooch on her. It screams, "That's right, folks, I'm the lucky sucker she's leaving with," which becomes a self-fulfilling prophecy.

- Include her in your conversations and stories, even if she's heard them before. This means eye contact or saying something like "Kirsten always thinks I'm making this part up, but it's true!"

- On the flip side, listen attentively when she tells a story or a joke, even if you've heard it a hundred times. This means no looking around or spacing out. Back her up as she's speaking; put your arm around her or offer up a "This is great" or "You'll love this" to the group. Your job is not to love the joke—your job is to be supportive.

- Make sure you introduce your GF. Sounds obvious, but you'd be surprised. And by the way, she'll love it when you introduce her to your friends and they say something like "At last. I'd heard so many fabulous things about you, I was beginning to think that Bill dreamed you up." So tell them stuff that will make them say that, and then reap the funky dividend.

- Your GF knows that no matter how much you love her, there are always going to be other babes to check out. Fine. We look, too. You're free to admire the eye candy when she's not around, but when you're together, just hold your head still and don't do it. Even if Eva Longoria walks by in a string bikini, don't ogle her in front of your GF. Trust us, it ain't worth it.

- And while we're on the topic of scoping, don't drown in the pool like your man Narcissus. Nothing's a bigger turnoff than a guy who checks himself out in every reflective surface he passes—store windows, the rearview, spoons, you name it. No girl wants to sleep with a guy who thinks he's hotter than she is.

- Standing up when your GF comes back to the table and opening the door for her may sound old-fashioned, but most girls love it. Same goes for the car door.

# CHAPTER 14

# RULES OF THE ROAD

***The car is a world unto itself. A form of transportation,*** a way to be out in public and yet totally alone, the car can be a form of therapy; a bedroom, an aphrodisiac, a whipping boy, a way to dominate, appease, piss off, show off, flip off; a form of mediation; a way to bond; a penis enhancer; a sad embarrassment; an extension of your true self; an extension of the self you hate; a burden that holds you back; a promise you can't live up to; a toy for your inner child; a haven from the world; a piece of shit you loathe; a way out; an escape.

No wonder you guys love your cars.

Your girlfriend probably won't care about your car the way you do, and she won't be able to recognize a 1954 Plymouth blah blah blah, even if it is cherry. But you're never going to get excited about an Italian handbag, so that makes us even. Maybe. You and your girlfriend are probably going to spend a lot of time in the car, and because each of you has your own issues when it comes to the way you drive (not to mention maintenance, music, cell phone use, and map reading), the car can be an incident waiting to happen. So pay attention to the road signs:

>  **Danger: Falling blood sugar**
>
>  **Caution: Cranky driver**
>
>  **Stay right, except to complain**

Be prepared and buckle up. That way, if you do hit a rough patch of road, the odds are pretty good that the two of you will make it out of there in one piece.

## Drivers Wanted

According to the BBC, men have an extra brain gene that females do not. No one is sure exactly what that extra gene does, but after extensive research on male behavior in vehicles, conducted in our secret laboratory (aka Patti's 1995 Honda Civic), we have determined that not only does it offer you guys the ability to hit fast-moving balls and parallel-park, this extra gene also dictates the type of driver you are.

> To your GF, being alone with you in your car feels like couples time. (Let's face it: To your GF, brushing your teeth feels like couples time.) But to you, it probably feels like a way to get things done, a way to get somewhere, or some precious space-out time. She wants to bond. You want to drive. We get it. We know we can be annoying, but we can't quite figure out what feels like couples time to you guys (except for sex), so we keep on trying.

- **Vin Diesel.** Some guys seem to take a testosterone pill when they get behind the wheel. They scream at other drivers, yell obscenities, and threaten to kick ass. You may think this forceful driving technique is manly, but your GF sees someone who should be driving to anger management classes, not the movies. Be Vin Diesel all you want on your own time, but when your GF is riding with you, take a chill pill.

- **Gilligan.** This is the guy who takes his GF out for a three-hour tour and leaves her shipwrecked by the side of the road. Your GF wants to feel you can take care of the situation, so before you go on a date, make sure the tank is full and that you know how to change a tire. If that's beyond you, then get a AAA card. Nothing makes a girl's libido go cold quicker than having to wait by the side of a road with her boyfriend who doesn't have an escape plan and couldn't tell a lug wrench from a tire gauge.

- **Felix.** Do you break into a sweat when your GF eats or spills something in the car? You may think you are just a guy who takes pride in his belongings and excellent care of his car, but actually, you're a Felix. To your GF, Felix behavior means that you care more about the condition of your upholstery than you do her comfort and enjoyment. Not exactly flattering. So do your antibacterial wipe-downs after you drop her off. (On the flip side, Pigpen Guy is also a turn-off. We don't want to compete for legroom with old McDonald's wrappers.)

- *Mario Andretti.* If you believe speed equals passion, chances are you also believe that the quickest way into your GF's pants is to drive there at 200 mph. She, on the other hand, is probably white-knuckling her way through the ride, wishing she'd found the time to make a will. So unless she specifically asks, "What has this thing got?" (indicating that you have found your soul mate), cut your speed in half and save the drag racing for your buddies.

- *Gearhead.* This guy can only talk about his ride. Even his GF's blank expression doesn't deter him from expounding on the double turbo, power traction, header, four-by-eleven monster tires, blah, blah, blah. You may see yourself as the ultimate guy, who can build a Ford out of spare radio parts, but she'll see you as that loser from auto shop whom she avoided in high school.

- *Fabio.* He considers his car a fashion accessory and his GF an adoring fan. He sees himself as a perfect Italian machine inside a perfect Italian machine. His GF sees a vain poseur who, at best, is going to get her killed by practicing his Tom Cruise smile in the rearview mirror and, at worst, is using every cubic inch under his hood to compensate for every cubic inch he doesn't have in his pants. If this sounds familiar, our only advice is to move to Europe.

## Dead End

Do you know why Moses was lost in the desert for forty years? He wouldn't stop for directions. We've heard all the jokes about men not asking for directions, and we're not going to repeat them here (except for that one, 'cause it's funny). It is an age-old quarrel: Men won't ask for them, women don't understand why. But we think you guys have been getting a bum rap in this department and that the whole issue has been misrepresented. It's not that guys hate asking for directions, it's that guys hate not being seen as competent and powerful. We don't blame you.

Your GF sees it differently. She doesn't think that asking for help is a sign of weakness; nor does she believe offering advice signals that she doesn't have faith in you. She sees it all as part of a caring partnership. Your GF wants you to stop and ask for directions because she is your teammate and is offering an assist. She doesn't realize her suggestion gets under your skin. It's not a big deal to her, it's just the two of you making your way in the world with a little bit of help from the gas station attendant. Your GF may not know it, but the most helpful thing she can say when you're lost is: "I know you'll get us there, honey." You guys deserve trust, encouragement, and admiration. Because ultimately, it's not about how long it takes you to find the IKEA, Pottery Barn, strip joint, whatever. It's about whether or not your GF—and the world, for that matter—sees you as a capable man. Her job is to give you the room and time to find your way. That said, when it's finally clear that you have no idea where you're going, your job is to suck it up and roll down your window.

## High Maintenance

While we're on the subject of capable men and their cars, we have to say a word about maintenance. Take our friend Betsey. She was having a heart-to-heart with her BF, Jeff. Her complaint? He didn't take care of her, didn't look after her needs. Why didn't he rub her shoulders after a long day at work? Why didn't he make dinner? How come he never bought her presents *just because*? Jeff couldn't believe his ears. "What are you talking about?" he said. "Who do you think changes the oil in your car? Refills the windshield-wiper fluid and the antifreeze? Who do you think checks your brakes? Look over here, honey, because it's me."

And there it was. When Betsey told the story, it was about her boyfriend dicking around in the garage on a Saturday afternoon when the two of them could be together at the movies. When Jeff told the story, it was about a Saturday afternoon spent taking care of his girl and being the best BF he knew how to be. He was nurturing her, cherishing her, and making sure she was safe, utilizing the skill set he had, albeit not in a way she could recognize. The way you offer and give of yourself is so foreign that sometimes we overlook the effort. We've said it before, we'll say it again: Reality is relative. One man's lube job is one woman's lovelorn afternoon.

## Backseat Drivers

You don't have to love her driving to love her, just like she doesn't have to love your weird red pants to love you (see chapter on clothes). Again, you have a choice. You can either correct her as she lets the clutch out too slowly or takes yet another wrong turn, or you can sit back and enjoy the ride, even if it takes a little longer to get there. Sometimes being right is not as important as being sweet.

If you don't feel safe, that's a whole different issue. How do you tell her to slow down without turning into Little Scaredy-Cat Man? Steer clear of sentences such as "You're making me nervous" or "What are you trying to do, kill us?" or "What the hell is wrong with you?" and stick with comments such as: "Is homicide a lifelong goal?" or "Is this car registered as a lethal weapon?" or "I like the idea of dying with two tons of metal wrapped around my lifeless limbs." With any luck, she'll get the message and slow the hell down, and you'll live to see your next birthday. And listen, fellas: Be smart. If you can't put up with anybody's driving but your own, get behind the wheel and let your girlfriend bitch about you.

Which she will.

Sometimes being a backseat driver is as irresistible to a woman as talking to her BF when he's on the phone with someone else. You know what we mean. You're trying to have a conversation, and she keeps interjecting: "Did you tell them we got dessert? What's so funny? Thank them for dinner. Did you say we're bringing friends?" All this while you're trying to talk to someone in Topeka. These background talkers are the same GFs who can't resist "helping" their BFs "get in the right lane," "slow down for the turn," or "remember the freeway is faster on Sundays." Background talkers equal backseat drivers.

We call it the three C's of backseat driving: correct, criticize, or complain. If either of you has the urge to indulge in the three C's, practice zipping it. If you can do it for only five minutes, that's okay; tomorrow you might make it to ten minutes. Then maybe you can have the quiet to space out or plan your next business move, and she will interpret the silence as meaningful time together. If she asks what you're thinking about, give her the classic fix-it-all statement: "I was thinking of you, honey. Just thinking about you." Then go back to your precious quiet time.

## Soft Shoulders and Dangerous Curves

***Cell phones in cars.*** We used to think call waiting was the only way to be rude to two people at once, but talking on your cell phone while driving with your significant other does the trick, too. We understand that the car doubles as an office and a chat room. It's a great place to catch up on phone calls. But it can cause a lot of fights, because the caller doesn't realize that his passenger feels frozen out. The fix isn't easy if you're addicted to your cell phone, but the rule is simple: If you are on a date, turn off your cell. If it is absolutely necessary to make or take a call, clear it with your passenger.

***Music in cars.*** What do you listen to and how? Most BFs like music in the car loud, with a capital "L." Chances are your GF likes it loud but not on the deafening, ear-splitting boy level. Maybe she likes to listen to talk radio and you'd rather have a root canal. You like to listen to Gangsta Rap, and she would rather have a Pap smear. We have no answer to this difference of taste except to share.

***Sex in cars.*** Just reading it is kind of hot, huh? But also a little uncomfortable. Basically, if you're under twenty-five you can get away with having sex in a car. It's sexy unless:

- Your car is a Mini. Or,

- It's a necessity because you still live with your mom and your car is the only place to get some. If you don't have anywhere else to go, spring for a hotel.

After the age of twenty-five, sex in a car should be the result of a special occasion or impulse, or when you:

- Are feeling particularly limber. Or,

- Have taken a Viagra and are trying to work off that legendary four-hour erection.

And, if you have a van, don't think it's okay to keep suggesting it. At best, you will seem like a perv stuck in the 1970s or, at worst, John Wayne Gacy's straight brother.

## *Driver's Ed*

Some of your best blow jobs will happen in the car; some of your worst fights, too. We can't tell you why, but some of your most important talks will also take place there. You know, the kind when you drive home, turn off the motor, and stay in the car talking another hour. We'd love to know how many proposals were made in the car, how many decisions to move in together, or how many breakups; how many of those long talks led to the realization that she is irredeemably crazy or that he is an incurable asshole. This is all assuming you don't live in NYC, where keeping a cab waiting for an hour would cost you a week's salary. A lot of your life happens in a car. Pivotal and pedantic. Good and bad. We've kept our guidelines few and simple. Follow them to ensure a smooth ride.

## Ten Things You Will Never Hear Your Girlfriend Say in the Car

1. I want to be on the road by nine.
2. The alignment is off.
3. Listen to that sucker purr.
4. This baby turns on a dime.
5. The temperature is perfect.
6. What I really want is a truck.
7. Listen to the bass on this subwoofer.
8. No, we don't have to stop, I peed at home.
9. I don't need the mirror, I already put on my makeup.
10. Can we listen to the end of the ball game?

## Ten Things She Will Never Hear You Say in the Car

1. You can put your mascara on in the rearview mirror if you want.
2. This heater makes it so cozy in here.
3. Look—light around the vanity mirror!
4. How far back does this seat go?
5. These tires are so big and fancy.
6. Look, there's room for all my stuff.
7. Convertibles are so unsafe.
8. I never wash my car.
9. I'm too old for a sports car.
10. I'm so glad we have this time alone.

# CHAPTER 15

# I NEED
# SPACE

## "My BF said he needed some space ...so I locked him outside. My BF said

he needed some space . . . so I threw the complete *Star Wars* DVD boxed set at his head. My BF said he needed some space . . . so I broke in to his place and stole his stereo, his big-screen TV, and his couch."

And so it goes.

The idea of space—his space, her space, our space—can mean so many things, none of them having to do with space, and all of them having to do with distance. The person uttering these three powerful words isn't asking for more legroom, he's asking for a new seat assignment, and more important, announcing that he's about to change rows. To a guy, space can be the final frontier: adventure and excitement, Klingons, holodecks, and cute alien girls with skimpy costumes. It can also be guy time, a chance for a beer with Spock and McCoy. But to your girlfriend, it can feel like she's being left in the *Enterprise* with the robot and the freeze-dried food.

Telling your GF that you need your space is like telling Superman that the Kryptonite is ready, and it can have the same detrimental effects: the same helplessness and fear. It can bring her to her knees. Always on the lookout for the hidden meaning, your girlfriend knows that "I need space" can mean almost anything, from "this is the night I play cards with the guys" to "this just isn't working, I need my freedom." She is afraid that your request for space actually means "I need out of here, away from you, it's been nice knowing you, adios, au revoir, auf Wiedersehen, don't let the door hit you on the way out." And do you know why she thinks this? Because it usually does.

## *Previously Owned Relationship*

People love to rename unpalatable facts with tasty nomenclature. "Used car" becomes "previously owned." "Jobless" becomes "between projects," and "short" becomes "vertically challenged." Sometimes your escape plan gets renamed as "just going out for a pack of smokes." Your GF may not speak man fluently, but over the years she has become good

### GPS—*Girlfriend Positioning System*

**"I need space."** Your girlfriend will panic when she hears those three little words, in much the same way as you panic when you hear "male pattern baldness."

at detecting the Heisman cloaked in a seemingly innocent phrase. She knows that "I need space" usually means:

- I really want to break up with you, but I haven't gotten up the nerve, so give me a few days, then I'll call and break up with you over the phone (or send you an e-mail if I'm a real coward).

- There's a cutie at work, and I need some time to see if I can trade you in for her.

- I find you suffocating and loathsome, but I am sure that is just my problem, so I can't say it directly.

- You're so great, I really should want to stay with you, but I don't, so maybe if I don't see you for a while, hopefully, I will miss you. If not . . . oh well.

- I need some time to talk to my friends about you—to confirm you're crazy—because I want out.

If you find yourself in this position and that sentence starts to bubble up from deep in your psyche or deep in your pants, stop! You are:

1. Trying to let her down easy.

2. Being a coward.

3. Trying to avoid a crash and the ensuing road burns.

4. All of the above.

Your concern, caution, and cowardice will only make things worse for your GF. So please, don't try to soften the blow. If you start treating your GF like a crime scene you need to run away from, she'll know something is wrong. (Also, everyone knows you walk away from a crime scene; otherwise everybody thinks you're guilty.) Don't try to weasel out of something. Tell her the truth. Just say:

1. "I don't want an exclusive relationship anymore."

2. "I really need to take a break for a while."

3. "This isn't working for me anymore."

4. "All of the above."

---

# Lame Excuses Used by Actual BFs in Real-Life Situations

·······································································

**HAL:*** "I need some space, my brother is getting jealous."

**MIKE:** "I need some space, I'm remodeling my apartment."

**DOUG:** "I need some space, I just . . . It's that . . . you know . . . I can't . . . no biggie."

**WILL:** "I need some space, work is really crazy right now."

**Every Tom, Dick, and Harry:** "I need some space, I've got a lot going on right now."

*\* Names have been changed to protect the innocent. Not really.*

## No Girls Allowed

We've known about your need for time with your friends since you hung that first KEEP OUT sign on your tree house. And sure, some GFs don't have a problem with guy time. They don't get their panties in a wad and mope around feeling blue, alone, and unloved. How mature. Then there are the rest of us.

We know that time with your friends is not the same as that mysterious appeal for space. We know that "guy time" and "I need space" are two completely different animals and that we should be okay with it. But here's the rub: A lot of BFs use this idea of time with their friends as an excuse to neglect their girlfriends. Your girlfriend is like a scavenger hunter looking for any clue that can tell her how you really feel. "Does he really just need some time, or is he tired of me? Is the basketball game that fun, or does he just not want to spend Sunday morning in my bed?" Why don't we believe you? Because in our formative years, our teenage BF would back off, feigning homework or baseball practice or a midterm (in July?), and the next thing you know, we'd see him at the mall with Robin Spielberg. And they weren't shopping.

Even those girlfriends who haven't been slammed by double-dipping can be hit by moments of immaturity and vulnerability. You take some guy time, and she starts to worry that the distance will give you time to reconsider, and that you'll decide she's not worth it, that she's not pretty enough, not interesting enough, not whatever enough. In other words, that you will come to your senses. And this is your problem because . . . ? It's not. We just want you to know what can come tagging along with your innocent need for time away.

Here's the irony: The more you pull away, the more your girlfriend will want to hang on to you. And the more freaked out she is by your time with the guys, the more you want it. It's human nature.

Here is what to do: You want time with the guys? Take it. Doesn't matter whether it's generic time with your pals or something specific: a poker night, a basketball game, or a road trip with your buddy. If you just need a break from all that estrogen, don't feel guilty. Take it. You can even be excited about it. We need breaks from testosterone, too. If a tsunami of resentment hits and you're met with a curt "sure," a terse "anything you want," a quivering lip, or a coffeepot thrown at your head, then it's time to take out your calculator and do the girl math:

Request for boy time + insecurity
    = a one-way ticket to Dumpsville.

If this is her sum total, balance her out with love and reassurance. Let her know that you're looking forward to seeing her and that you'll give her a call as soon as you finish your game of one-on-one, your knitting class, your five-county dirt-bike tour, or [insert activity here].

On the other hand, she may have a legitimate gripe, which means this has nothing to do with insecurity or self-esteem issues and everything to do with the fact that you haven't been spending enough time with her. If this is the case, don't cancel your guy time. Just make room for girlfriend time so she'll know it's coming and she can relax.

(Of course, there's always the possibility that you're lying. You're dressing up "I need space" in the misleading costume of poker night. If this is the case, see above guidelines, because you want out.)

If none of these scenarios is applicable and your girlfriend still resents your poker night, Sunday-morning basketball game, or drinks at the pub, ask her to read this section and back off. Tell her that your taking the time you need is good for the two of you and that she should give you her blessing for guy time in the same way that you give your blessing for girl time.

## GIRL ON GIRL
### Advice for Your Girlfriend!
...............................

If you let your boyfriend off the leash a little, his desire to run away might just go away. If it doesn't, you were never going to keep him in the first place. Leave him for the dog catcher.

## Space Invaders

If your girlfriend is over the age of fourteen (and we hope for your sake she is), she knows that every BF needs time to himself—every GF, too, for that matter. So if you want guy time, go for it. If you need time alone, take it. When you don't want to spend the night—too tired, too much to do the next day, need a break, just don't want to—then don't. But know there is a tollbooth on this road. You have to throw in communication and attention before you can be on your way to a breezy afternoon of golf, an evening of badminton, a day with your Scrabble club, or whatever else you guys like to do. Take the time you need and feel good about it, because believe us, nothing is worse than being with a guy who would rather be somewhere else.

# CHAPTER 16

# SEX

***Here it is—the chapter most of you probably turned to first.*** Sorry, there aren't any pictures. Not that you need them. But this chapter has something you do need: the inside scoop straight from the horse's mouth. Pay attention, because a man who truly grasps the principles outlined in this chapter will have his girlfriend eating out of the palm of his hand. Or whatever. Stick with us, slugger, and we'll help you step up to the majors.

Okay. Here's the first big secret. We don't always admit it, but in many ways we're just like you. We like sex as much as you do. We may not think of it as often (on average, men think of sex every fifty-two seconds), and maybe not in the same way, but we think about it very deeply. For the most part, we're every bit as horny and dirty-minded. We talk graphically among ourselves about our likes and dislikes. And yes, we talk about how you are in bed.

The second big secret? We're also completely different. Sound like a contradiction? It is. We're not just saying this to torture or confuse you. It's confusing enough without any help from us. Sure, we get turned on by many of the same naughty, lascivious, blatantly sexual things that you do, but those things often seem to be all you need to send your stallion tearing out of the gates at full gallop. And that's where we're different. That stuff only gets us to the track and maybe trots us around the ring a few times. We need the other stuff, too, the stuff you may not think of because you aren't built to need it as much as we do.

For most of us, the other stuff is key. We want to be tearing around that track, matching you stride for stride—we want that as much as you do—but it's the other stuff that gets us there. And for women, it's all about *how* you get there.

## The Other Stuff

So what is this other stuff? Don't worry. As always, we will put this in terms you can readily understand: A woman's sexuality is like a home entertainment center. You feel a little better already, don't you?

Each home entertainment system comes with its own set of directions, power cords, and buttons to push. And so it is with your girlfriend. Unfortunately, she's harder to install and doesn't come with instructions. But if you simply take a moment and study the newly unboxed components that are laid out before you, you will sense the first tiny connections that must be made. If nothing pops out at you, simply ask. You'd be surprised how communicative many home entertainment systems can be.

Every GF has her own factory settings, basic defaults, and presets, but rare is the model who has a sex-on-demand feature, or a convenient fast-forward button that lets you bypass the corny dialogue so you can head straight to the hard-core action. Your girlfriend can store countless hours of programming, so you've got to consider the whole lineup; that is, what's going on in the rest of her life. If she's distracted or under stress, give her time to relax and decompress before making your move. Better yet, help her relax. You never know, you may be lucky enough to have the type of GF who likes nothing better than to wind down by going down.

Before turning your girlfriend on, you should know that her power source comes from feeling connected to you. Without this intimacy, she probably won't want to have sex. Most GFs will plug in to a power source in a very specific way. This is a safety feature; if not used properly she will shut down. It doesn't mean that a quickie is out of the question; it doesn't mean you have to talk after sex; and it doesn't mean that sex has to be serious. It can be wacky, kinky, and fast, but first she needs to be plugged in. To you.

## BE PREPARED

**Women prefer thirty to forty minutes of foreplay (as any cookbook will tell you, it's best to preheat the oven before you put in the roast), while men are content with thirty to forty seconds (which is enough time to put a TV dinner in the microwave). Your suggestion that we go back to your place, though charming, does not count as foreplay.**

## *A Kiss Is Just a Kiss*

Not on your life. Great kissing is essential. For women, it's probably the single greatest turn-on. If you already have this one down, congratulations and happy hunting. If not, then it's about time you stepped up your game. Trust us, you'll be glad you did. Women gossip for years about boyfriends who were lame kissers.

Kissing is an art form and, as such, comes in many different styles and genres: the peck, the passionate kiss, the teasing kiss, the foreplay kiss, the postcoital kiss, the "I can't wait to see you later kiss," the "I want to throw you down on the ground right here kiss." There are kisses for almost every occasion, but for now let's focus on the passionate, romantic kiss, the one that either can be a complete experience unto itself or the lead-in to other things.

Some say great kissers are born, not made, but we don't believe that. If you are that great kisser waiting to be discovered, here are some tips. Start gently. Your lips have the power to woo and seduce. Think of them as emissaries charged with communicating your most tender feelings. Everything you want her to know can be communicated when your lips meet. Caress her lips with your lips. Does that sound cheesy? It won't when you see what it does to her. Pretend you're not going to go any further than the kiss. That way you'll be more likely to take the time she needs. And don't forget that it's not a lip-lock you're after. Touch her face gently with your hands, or wrap your arms around her. After a few minutes of this, it may be time for The Tongue to make his entrance.

Sure, sometimes in a passionate moment, the tongue can be your opening number, but more often than not he needs a warm-up act. So introduce your tongue to her mouth the way you might introduce your body to a cold-water pond: Inch your way in slowly, don't jump in all at once. And though some serious tonguing can be nice, don't perform an oral exam or she'll start to feel like she's at the dentist.

These are only suggestions. Your girlfriend may be into something completely different. How will you know? Ask her. When she answers, be receptive. She'll let you know when you get it right. A good kisser is hard to find and even harder to leave. Here are some hints on lip management—in other words, the types of kisses you want to avoid:

- **The Saint Bernard.** No lips, all tongue, drool everywhere.

- **Dead Man Smooching.** Like getting mouth-to-mouth from someone who drowned last week: limp, flat, everything wimpy.

- **The Leapin' Lizard.** A long, pointy tongue that slides everywhere as if it's looking for a fly. Feels like being kissed by some creepy high school principal.

- **The Guppy.** Like being kissed by one of those fish you watch cleaning the tank in your dentist's office.

- **The Grinder.** Great kissing is not achieved by grinding your teeth into hers. No.

- **The Frito-Lay/Starbucks/Caesar Salad.** A bad lunch or snack choice can lead to toxic breath. Mints are not just candy, you know.

---

# Talk to Me, Baby . . .

In the same way your GF must tell you her likes and dislikes, you have a right and a duty to let her know what works for you. This goes for everything from blow jobs to back rubs to oatmeal. We want and appreciate the information, especially if it's offered in a loving way. When explaining what you like, don't reference the woman who made your eyes roll back in your head by name. If pressed, say something like "It was so long ago, baby, I can't even remember who it was." She'll know you're lying, but she'll forgive you. Look, it's possible she's secure enough that those disclosures won't come back to haunt you, but until you're sure, why take the chance?

---

## Female Erogenous Zones

When you decide that you care about her, then you're going to want to give her pleasure. The best way to be able to do that is by becoming an expert on her body. So here they are, in descending order—your girlfriend's erogenous zones:

**The mind.** Face it. Nothing turns us on more than the stuff you say, the way you talk to us, being funny or charming, and those rare moments when you actually perceive what we want and need. Really listen to us, and you're in for a hell of a night. This is the big one. Everything else is a distant second.

**The ears.** A weak spot if ever there was one. Talking and whispering can be very effective. A little blowing in the ear is good, too. Try a little sexy talk. Licking is also good, but if she smacks the side of her head afterward like a waterlogged swimmer, you might be getting carried away. Nibbling gently on the lobes can be nice, but pull a Mike Tyson, and vengeance will be swift and ugly.

**The neck.** This one is very important. Fingers, tongue, bring it on. Some nibbling is okay, especially at the nape of the neck, under the hair. Yum. One hickey's cool. Two is definitely too many.

**Breasts.** Thought they'd be higher on the list, didn't you? They're not. Here's the thing about breasts: Don't squeeze them too hard. They're not udders, for God's sake. They're boobs, and, just like us, they want to be stroked, appreciated, and adored, though some uneducated louts treat them like an old-fashioned radio, twisting the dials and pushing the buttons. Yes, we know they get you in the mood, but don't forget they're actually attached to our bodies. Nipple sensitivity varies wildly, so take it slow and pay close attention to her responses. Some gals have nipples you could go at with a belt sander and they'd barely flinch. (Impressed with the power-tool reference, aren't you?) With others, a cool breeze is almost more than they can bear.

And while we're on the subject, love big boobs? Guess what? Smaller ones are usually more sensitive. And while we're on the subject, whether our bra runneth over or our cup is half empty (whatever the Good Lord or the Good Surgeon provided), let us think it's your preference. We might know you're full of it, but we'll definitely forgive you.

**Secret spots.** Every woman has a secret hot spot. They may seem odd or secondary, but find the right spot on the right girl in the right moment, and it will pay a huge dividend. Some of our faves include the inside of the forearm, the small of the back, the back of the knee, the feet—top and bottom—the ass . . . cheeks are great, and . . . well, use your discretion. As you're exploring, keep an eye out for goose bumps. They usually indicate you're doing something right. What else? Oh, baby . . . underarms, especially if they've just been shaved. Run your fingers lightly over her skin. The lighter the touch, the more delicious.

We are breaking it down for you, but the truth is, there isn't one thing and one thing alone that lights her match. We wish it were as simple as "Nibble on her thorax and she's on her back counting ceiling tiles." Unlike you, women respond to things as a whole: The seduction has to be complete. What turns her on most of all is when you deal with the entire package.

And speaking of packages, when we want you, we want you body and soul. Not just Mr. Winky.

## The Clitoris: A User's Guide

This brings us to the sacred temple. That's right, we're talking about the elusive, perennial all-star . . . The Clitoris. You've heard about it, you've read about it, you may have even seen one in the wild. Pay close attention. The clitoris is a trick question. By that we mean there is no right answer. Forming a loving relationship with your woman's clitoris will be the ultimate test. Because like her cousin the nipple, Ms. Clitoris is *a little different on everyone.*

### Frequently Asked Questions

**Where is that sucker?** Good question. Some people have trouble with this, though to be honest, we're not completely sure why. At the top of the vagina itself, where the labia or lips come together in an upside-down "V," right there—the clitoris can be found under that fold of soft, sensitive skin. Sometimes it's even peeking out a bit, but not too often. It's usually covered from the top by a tiny cloak of pink skin. That's the clitoral hood. Be nice to her, she's your friend.

**Now that I've found it, what do I do?** Now the tricky work begins. What works for one woman will put another on the ceiling with her nails dug into the plaster. Here's a basic strategy for dealing with a clitoral first date: Think of the clitoris as a really hot, fancy chick who recently moved into the neighborhood. The guy who goes racing right up to the door usually gets nowhere. Walk by a few times. Circle the house. Then leave. Drive by again later. Real slow. Let her know you're in the neighborhood. When she's starting to think you may not be interested, introduce yourself. But not to her. Spend a little time getting to know her neighbors. Stay close by, and when the time feels right, send her messages through labial intermediaries. If she wants you to make contact directly, she'll let you know. And if you do make direct contact, be alert. If it's too much for her, she'll pull back a little or give a quick intake of breath. Don't be afraid to check in here; sometimes the sounds she makes that mean "Please don't touch me there yet" are astonishingly similar to the sounds that mean "Don't stop or I'll tear your ears off."

Sometimes she will gently steer you to the area she wants you to work on. Often one side of the power button is more sensitive than the other. This varies from woman to woman and sometimes from week to week with the same woman. Hardly seems fair, but what are you gonna do? She might ask, nudge, or pant that she needs it a little different than before. Think of it as a new frontier with a familiar landscape.

**The home stretch.** When she is approaching the promised land, she will get very focused and intense, and her body may shake or tighten up, particularly the muscles around the desired location. At this point, don't change what you're doing or get creative. Keep it steady and bring her on home. Be patient. She can hover in that spot, paddling like hell to catch the wave for what can feel like endless minutes. Hang in there. It'll be worth the wait.

After your girlfriend sings hallelujah, don't stop your ministrations immediately. She can become super-sensitive after orgasm, but keep going, and wait for her to stop you. Often there'll be a lovely, albeit brief period when she'll want to come down slowly. We know a lot of guys have a powerful urge to collapse or even pass out, but if you can fight through that and guide her back to earth with a warm, loving touch, she will be very grateful. And who knows? You might find yourself in an unexpected rematch.

# *The G-Spot*

For some women this magic spot is as easy to locate as Las Vegas. For others, it's more like the lost city of Atlantis. The G-spot really does exist, though, and it's worth getting acquainted with it. If your GF knows where her camp is set up, get her to show you what you need to know. And if she doesn't, then you need to take a wilderness tour together. That may seem awkward or perhaps labor-intensive, but it's worth the effort, because the "G" in "G-spot" stands for all GOOOOD.

***Sounds harder than calculus.*** It is, but the guys who stuck with calculus are being very well compensated today. And you will be, too. If you need additional tutoring, watch your GF masturbate. You'll see that she probably gets some heat going with her little friend by moving and stroking the skin all around it. When it's your turn, pay close attention to her breathing and the sounds she makes. That should let you know how you're doing. She'll be flattered by the effort you're making and will seek to help you out. It's a win-win.

## The Size of Your Boat

Dear Lord, the hang-ups that can get going around this one. Yes, it's true, some women do prefer the larger yachts, but the fact is, most of us don't care too much one way or the other. As long as you have a boat that floats and you're willing to make your GF the exclusive passenger, then she will find a way to make it work. Some women actually prefer a rowboat to a lengthy motor yacht for reasons of comfort, and because the rowboat captain often puts more time and effort into developing his piloting skills, i.e., the motion of the ocean. By the way, if you're one of those skippers who has succumbed to the temptation to give your water craft a cute or boastful name, you might want to consider keeping that to yourself, so if the relationship doesn't work out, you don't run the risk of walking into a bar and being greeted with "Well, if it isn't Mr. Wondernoodle!"

## Soup to Nuts

What follows is a veritable smorgasbord of saucy topics that invariably rear their heads.

### Oral Sex

*Giving.* We know some men are squeamish about going down on their GFs, but we think that's a lack of confidence. It can be a satisfying experience all on its own, or a superb way to tease her into a state where she's begging you to consummate the act. She will appreciate your obvious comfort with this most intimate part of her body, and she will show that appreciation with the most intimate parts of yours. As for technique, we suggest you read the above section on the clitoris. Now read it again.

*Getting.* Gee, what to say here? Most of you seem okay with receiving oral sex, but as you may have figured out by now, we're simply not wired in such a way to generally enjoy this outside of an intimate, lovemaking context. That doesn't mean the occasional while-you're-driving blow job is out of the question, but giving you head while you take in a playoff game usually is. Tell her what you like, but no matter how turned on you get, don't shove on the back of her head. EVER. If you luck into one of those rare women who are born without a gag reflex, congratulations, you're a lottery winner. Most women have one, and pushing her head down on you is likely to set it off. And what a bummer that is. We know teeth-on-penis accidents are a real drag, and we try like hell to avoid them, but if we give you a nip, let us know, and together we can create a safe playroom for your little fella. Right, sorry. Your *big* fella. To swallow or not to swallow? This is your GF's decision; sperm tastes like Clorox, so we're sure you can understand if she chooses not to.

### Orgasms

Some women have half a dozen orgasms through straight intercourse every time they climb in the ring. Others need to help things along with manual stimulation (either directly or indirectly) of the clitoris. Some women huff and puff like the Big Bad Wolf and climax with one great big earth-shattering orgasm, while others squeak out a dozen little baby ones. You'll soon learn which type your girlfriend is. And who knows? You could have fun trying to expand the boundaries of her experience.

Some women you will meet are what's called nonorgasmic; it's just like whistling, some people never learn how to do it. If you fall for a nonorgasmic woman and you're both up to the challenge, you can make pursuit of an orgasm a project. This requires great sensitivity, patience, and communication. It may require a joint effort over a number of weeks. As we said, if you're into her, it can be a bonding and intimate task that, once accomplished, may leave her feeling pretty grateful.

### Anal Sex

For some folks, this is still a big taboo—which can make it sexy. It's a very personal choice. It's definitely not an issue you should force, and it's probably best to let some time pass before you go there. If the decision is made in favor of a back-door invasion, start very slowly, and gradually work your way up from fingers. Lubrication is a must. Wait until everyone's feeling all scrubby and clean. Big rule: Anything that touches the ass must not touch the puss. Not unless you want her to have a slamming urinary tract infection that'll put her out of action for a week or more.

### Threesomes

If we want to do this, we'll let you know. There's nothing more tiresome than a guy dropping enormous hints all the time. Okay, there may come a day when we actually want to drag someone to bed with us, but if it's a woman, she won't be the vacant bimbo from the health club with huge fake tits whom you've been fantasizing about. It'll probably be that slender brunette from yoga class, and be careful, because if you're not the cunning linguist you think you are, you're about to get shown up. Also, we might want to invite your sexy best friend, Titus. So think about that before you suggest inviting ours.

### Waxing/Shaving Pubic Hair

Don't. Unless we specifically ask you to. A little neat trimming for unruly or runaway bush is okay, but anything more makes you look like a dildo. As a rule, steer clear of anything that reminds us of that affordable and less annoying option that never leaves the seat up and doesn't snore. And when we shave or wax, it's just like any other haircut we get—*notice it.* It hurt like hell, and we want a little appreciation for our effort.

### Talking During Sex

This is a lot like talking during life: It's all about what you say and when you say it. And, of course, about knowing when to shut up and go to work. Some dirty stuff is nice, but context is everything. If it's our first time together, "Take it all, bitch" might spoil the mood. (Actually, that could spoil the mood anytime.) Also, you should be sure that there's an "all" for us to "take." It's generally a good idea to steer away from purple prose. Only refer to your "throbbing love missile" if you're looking for some belly laughs. Something like "You're so fucking beautiful" is a good segue into naughty talk. If we join in, consider it a green light. If we don't, proceed with caution.

### Sex Toys

At certain junctures in the relationship, the introduction of some mutually approved appliances can be a good thing.

However, we don't want to feel like a surge protector that's so overstuffed as to represent a fire hazard. One at a time, gently, and for God's sake, don't show up with one of those horse cocks that are on display at sex shops unless you plan to use it on a female horse. Also, if you're going to bring a vibrator, don't get one that's too expensive or effective, or the next time you do something asinine (which will be soon), your usefulness may be called into question (see below).

### Masturbation

By all means, knock yourself out. We love it, too. But it better not come out of our check, if you know what we mean. A little hint: Once in a great while, if we don't want to have sex but we seem a little on the fence about it, start gently stroking your man quietly in the bed next to us. (Unless we have to be up early. In that case, go to sleep, you inconsiderate slob.) Sometimes an occasional glance at the way you pleasure yourself can be an enticing and informative teaser.

### Pornography

We haven't been interested in pornography the way you have since the ninth grade. So don't put on *Doing Miss Daisy* and expect us to get immediately turned on. You might even be introducing your GF to pornography, in which case take it slow, Daddy-o, or she may think you're too pervy (a little pervy's okay) or that she's not enough for you.

## Assume the Position

Since humans began having sex, they have constantly sought ever more creative positions in which to perform the act. Maybe it's the desire for newness, or maybe it's the never-ending quest for another variation on that wonderful feeling.

Imagine you are playing Twister, and see what fits where. This can be good clean fun as long as you don't injure something and you're prepared to see each other from some potentially unflattering angles. It can also be useful in finding those positions you both enjoy and which suit the mechanics of how your two bodies fit together. We had a friend who dated an energetic fellow she called The Yogi. This guy felt the need to cycle through so many poses, she felt like she had unknowingly joined Cirque du Soleil.

# Safety First

We are all grown-ups—what can we say? Have safe sex. Don't be stupid. Not only are STDs at an astronomical high, but just go hang around any of your friends or relatives who have kids. There is no better advocacy for birth control than spending an afternoon with a two-year-old. And if that isn't challenge enough, think of this: Any man can look sexy putting a condom on but it takes a big man to look sexy taking it off.

### Postcoital Behavior

We know it's an effort to act like you're still interested after you've gotten off. For some of you, it's an effort to stay awake (all those crazy sex chemicals). But for your GF, it's the most important time. So don't check out yet. A little cozy cuddling time goes a long way. Take a deep breath and spend an extra ten minutes, and hang out. You will need to practice this.

## Sex Education

Sex is the beginning and the end of the story. It's the thing that brings people together and the thing that breaks them apart. When a relationship gets rocky, sex is the first thing to go and the last thing to come back. For BFs, sex is a way to be and stay connected; in fact, sex is the guy's dictionary of love. All the words you could ever need or possibly want are embedded within its covers. Women want to be and stay connected, too, but sex is not their dictionary of love so much as their thesaurus. There are other choice words out there that we can use, other ways we can express our love and lust for you, but ultimately, finding that perfect bon mot seals the deal. We haven't covered all the bases—it's a big subject (if you're lucky), so we've just touched on a few highlights.

We all want excitement, satisfaction, relaxation, release, connection, and fun. Sure, there will be times when certain communications between us are lost in translation: She says "tomahto" and you say "tomato"; she says "faster" and you hear "bastard"; she says "No, higher" and you hear "Use pliers." She says "Back that truck up off my labia" and you hear "I hear Tony Blair's in Saudi Arabia." Don't worry. Sex is a language and every woman you are with will speak her own particular dialect. As you begin to learn hers she will be catching on to yours. Did you ever think learning a language could be this fun? So much better than high school Spanish.

> **A hook you can hang your hat on: If you want sex, fix something.**

# What's Sexy to Your Girlfriend

Bringing her a cup of coffee in the morning

Clean sheets

Back rubs

Watching her as she takes off her shirt

When she wears your shirts with nothing under them around the house

Talking to her when she is in the tub

Standing up when she comes back to the table

Keeping your eye on her when you are at a party

When you put her in a taxi and tell the cabbie "take care of my GF"

Holding her hand

Cooking dinner, whether you're good at it or not

Dorkiness

Men who like kids

Being a good athlete

Being a bad athlete

A white T-shirt

A man who makes fun of himself

Knowing a foreign language

A great kisser

Being a great traveler

Confidence

Being good to your mother

Being generous

Wearing glasses

# CHAPTER 17

# I HATE
## HOW YOU
## CHEW

***The first three to six months with your GF constitute*** the honeymoon period. Romantic dinners, long walks on the beach, afternoons spent lying in bed with the paper. It's a time of perfection, the days of wine and roses when a trip to the grocery store presents yet another opportunity to kiss, let her marvel at your wit, bask in her adoration, and dream of sex on the kitchen table. Lust and romance leave no opportunity for anything that isn't exciting.

As time passes and you have some breathing room between sex and obsession, you start to notice some annoying things about her. Small things, like the fact that she leaves the cap off the toothpaste or misplaces the remote. You ignore that faint alarm going off in your head. You push the snooze button. Twice. But as more time goes by and the alarm gets louder, it becomes harder to brush aside her annoying habit of laughing when she's nervous, or her surprising ability to slurp her white wine. It becomes a burr under your saddle, a hitch in your gait, a fly in your soup, a poop at your party, a harsh to your mellow, a pain in your ass. It happens to everyone. No two people have a perfect, smooth joining. We are humans, not Lincoln Logs.

Right about this same time, we guarantee your GF is starting to hear a buzz of her own.

She notices when you leave wet towels on the bed, tuck your shirts into your underwear, interrupt her when she's talking on the phone (even though she does it to you), and trim your toenails on the couch, leaving small piles of clippings between the cushions. But there's a difference. You guys are a lot better at riding through the momentary annoyances than we are. A pebble dropped in the girl pond will cause ripples all the way to the shore. When a pebble drops in the boy pond, the water absorbs it; the surface doesn't change at all. You guys seem able to carry a bigger load of irritants than we can. We've seen it countless times. The BF shrugs, shakes his head, and files it under "Oh Well," that big category made up of a lot of manila folders, all of which are bulging and ripping at the seams. Sure, eventually, you guys lose your cool, but you take longer than we do. Ladies first.

## Sum of All Things

The fact that you do things that annoy her, or that she does things that annoy you, will concern your GF. She will interpret it as discord, which will upset her, and she will respond in a way that seems way out of proportion to the situation. It's not a linear equation, it's Girl Math, and it goes something like this:

- He doesn't smile at the waiter = He's not kind, we have no future.

- He eats all the Junior Mints before the movie starts = He's selfish, we have no future.

- He sucks lobster out of its shell = He's gross, we have no future.

- He's late because his car had a flat tire = He didn't want to pick me up, we have no future.

- He keeps describing movies to me that we saw together = He doesn't notice I exist, we have no future.

- He didn't take a shower before our date = He's not excited to see me, we have no future.

- If I really loved him, I wouldn't notice this stuff = I might not love him, we have no future.

- I can tell he's annoyed when I drink white wine = He doesn't want me to have fun, we have no future.

- He hates that it takes me forever to come to a decision = I'm already annoying him, just wait till I let crazy out of the bottle, we have no future.

Since your GF finds the sum of all this troubling, she will bring it to your attention so that you can fix it. Once you fix it, she thinks it won't trouble her anymore. And then her Girl Math will look something like this:

- He stopped sucking lobster = We have a future.

- He stopped being mean to the waiter =
  We get along perfectly.

- He stopped eating all the treats = He loves me.

- He bought me shoes *I love* = He sees my true being.

- He is actually listening = I fascinate him.

- He remembered my cat's birthday =
  I'm the center of his universe.

## *Your Girlfriend's Girlfriends*

Your girlfriend needs her girlfriends. She needs to spend time with them and talk to them on the phone—a lot. She will be talking about you.

Get used to the idea that these few select girls will know *all* your secrets. Don't get in the way. Encourage it—even if you don't understand it—because if she isn't getting her girlfriend fix you're going to have to step in and be a substitute girlfriend, and do a lot of talking about feelings. With any luck you'll like her friends and they'll like you. But sometimes it's not so easy. If you don't get along, tread lightly; those packs of gal-pals can do a lot of damage if they are not on your side. Either way, they are a big part of your girlfriend's life and a big part of your life with her.

## Chew on This

So she tells you and she tells you and she tells you about all the things you do that bother her. To her, this is valuable information that will stop you from being rude or annoying or nerdy, and stop her from having to find a new BF. To you, it is nagging. And we agree. There is no such thing as constructive criticism. Ever. It is a poisonous concept. It's not that we can't all improve ourselves in one way or another; it's that whatever small gains are made get buried under a mound of resentment. So what should you do if your GF just keeps picking at you? First, inform her that she is indeed nagging, not being helpful, not giving priceless advice, but nagging with a capital "N," and that there is a reason "nagging" rhymes with "gagging." If she keeps it up, as a last resort, line up your own list of annoyances, because it sounds like she needs your assistance getting down off her high horse. Are any of these in your stable of complaints?

- She throws her jeans in the washing machine with sixty dollars in the pocket.

- Her mom is her best friend and knows way too much about your relationship.

- She never pays her bills on time and then is pissed when she is charged a penalty for being late.

- After one drink, she starts to speak with a slight British accent (think Madonna).

- She believes the most expensive is always the best (i.e., restaurants, doctors, car mechanics).

- She rides the clutch.

- She insists on wearing Crest Whitestrips to bed.

- She loses her car keys in the depths of her crap-filled purse and asks you accusingly what you did with them.

- She tries to make friends with every waiter.

- Nothing is simple for her. She can't make a decision and stick to it.

- She is moody and critical and takes everything personally.

- The electronics in your house baffle her, and she thinks you did it on purpose.

## GIRL ON GIRL
### Advice for Your Girlfriend!

There's small stuff, medium stuff, and big stuff. Stop trying to improve your fella in the first two categories. It won't work. Save your nagging for the big stuff. Think practice makes perfect? Then practice the perfection of appreciation.

# *Farting*

Air attack. Blanket bomb. Bottom burp. Putt-putt. Windy pop. Barking spiders. Whatever you call it, introduce the idea of farting slowly. Each GF will respond to your presentation in her own way. We have a friend who charges her BF a dollar every time he farts in bed; she's made a pretty penny since they started dating, almost enough for a digital camera. We feel she has every right to collect, since she is on the receiving end. He maintains he would only fart in bed with a woman he loves and is committed to. She should be flattered.

## *Airing Your Dirty Laundry in Public*

A lot of people find an outlet for their daily aggravations by saving them up and then waiting to air them in front of other people. You know the carping that some couples do? Making a joke about how she's always late, how he never remembers anything, how she can't balance her checkbook, how he always whistles after taking a poop. At the beginning of a relationship, people do this to show the world their great connection: "Look at us. We're so cute and so close that we can say anything to each other." That's why people observing it (the people the display is for) find it both distasteful and yet enviable. Distasteful because, well, *yuck*. Enviable because the grousing duo is so intimate and so comfortable nestled in their "Team Us" (and they're not even wearing matching jackets).

The problem is that this quick bridge to intimacy can be treacherous, because public jocular nitpicking very quickly becomes the only safe forum to air daily aggravations. What starts out as unifying becomes erosive, and like acid rain, it will eventually corrode the lovely details of your relationship, leaving you with an ugly gray lump of grievances. We believe this type of grousing should be reserved for old married couples who have earned the right not to stand each other.

Keep your fault-finding private: It's unattractive and damaging. Daily aggravations are like weeds, and if they're choking your ability to enjoy each other, you've got to yank them out by the roots or they'll take over the whole garden.

## *Your Last Nerve*

When it comes to weathering annoying habits, you guys can carry a bigger load than we can, and for a longer time, before it starts to feel heavy. But after a while that weight does your back serious damage, and rather than tell your GF to knock it off, you suffer in silence. Then, much to our surprise, you run off with your physical therapist. A woman's response is exactly the opposite. While you're willing to put up with too much for too long, she overreacts to small annoyances because her sense of proportion is off. That works in your favor when you tell her twelve inches is about the length of your finger, but not so well when she decides that your inability to wash toothpaste spit off the sink means your relationship is doomed. It's like we are nearsighted. If it's close enough to focus on, it must be a big deal. We both need to take a page out of each other's book, because you guys don't know when to cry uncle, and we GFs haven't learned to Hang Ten.

## The Tip of the Iceberg

Sometimes that peak of annoyance popping out is actually part of a vast continent of ice below the surface that no one sees but you feel. Maybe the reason you're bugged that she takes two hours at the ATM (what is she doing—her taxes?) is that you're still steaming over a past grievance. Or maybe you're done with her, done with being her BF, done with the whole relationship.

How do you separate being anal, controlling, or just plain pissy from listening to that inner voice telling you to jump ship? Take the FDI test: Frequency, Duration, Intensity. (In your less gentlemanly moments, "FDI" can also stand for "*F*ucking *D*rives me *I*nsane.") On a scale from one to ten, rate the annoying occurrences—hogging the covers, playing with her hair, saying "You've got to be kidding" forty-six times a day. If your GF is consistently scoring perfect tens, you are not the winner on *Dancing with the Stars*, you are the runaway bride. Don't fool yourself. You want out. So get out. (You have our permission to skip ahead to the section on breaking up.)

## *And Speaking of Annoyances . . .*

There's Greenwich mean time, daylight saving time . . . and girlfriend time. This is the oldest one there is. You ask your GF when she's going to be ready, and she says five minutes. It will always be ten. Or more. Sorry. We wish we could tell you why we do this, but we can't. There always seems to be one more thing to do that will make us look better. And that's what we all want, isn't it? We know it drives you crazy. That's why we let you have the armrest on the airplane.

On the other hand, if you take the FDI test and results are inconclusive but you still find yourself thinking, "Does she have to put her lipstick on in the rearview mirror?" or "Could she remember where she parked her car just once?" or "Is she physically unable to keep a phone call under two minutes?," please tell her. Not every little thing or every little time—life's too short for that. But don't pretend you're okay with things when you're not. It's only a matter of time before that molehill turns into a mountain. Okay, you may like mountain climbing, but there will come a day when you don't want to lug all your gear around anymore, and that's the day you'll check out on your GF. Literally. Register your complaint and see if your irritation evaporates. If it disappears, then good for you. Welcome to the wonderful world of working things out with another human being.

# CHAPTER 18

# LOVE HURTS

***Our friend Hilary is afraid to fly, though she travels a lot.*** An otherwise intelligent and rational woman, she has no problem understanding that when she's in her car, she will occasionally hit potholes and patches of rough road. But all reason leaves her when she's in a plane. She freaks out at every bump, certain she's going to crash and burn. One day, as luck would have it, she found herself seated next to an airline pilot on a trip to Colorado. The flight was rough, and she clutched her armrest and admitted she was terrified of turbulence. That's when Chuck Yeager stepped in: "Airplanes cruise on highways of air currents, which are turbulent by their very nature. Bumps aren't an exception to an otherwise smooth ride; the bumps *are* the ride." Not only was he cute, his reassurance offered her a new perspective, a much better way to fly the friendly skies. This new understanding, combined with a prescription of Xanax, made Hilary one relaxed passenger.

Think of your GF as a nervous traveler whose sense of proportion goes out the window when it comes to the day-to-day bumps in your relationship. A heated discussion will feel like a fight to her, and a fight will feel like you, as a couple, are about to crash and burn. Your girlfriend regards an argument as unexpected turbulence, and she's terrified that the two of you won't be able to withstand the shaking. Not to mention her concern that the refreshment cart will be put away, and where's the fun in that?

It's not that your girlfriend is a sissy. It's that she's afraid of what the friction means. Sure, there are a lot of women out there who love a good tussle, but when it comes to matters of the heart, most of us use a magnifying glass. That means small issues seem huge, and often we can't see them any other way. Men can enjoy a heated discussion on almost any subject and approach it like a good workout: It's healthy

## BE PREPARED

Women exaggerate everything because we feel everything on an exaggerated level. A lot of it is hormonal, and we're not kidding. Testosterone allows you guys to go through life like an aircraft carrier busting through the waves on an even keel and at an even speed. Estrogen makes us feel like a little rowboat. We are riding the waves, yes, but we feel every bump, every crest and swell. By explaining this, we are not giving ourselves a gender Get Out of Jail Free card, we're just offering insight into your GF's behavior. She is hyper-tuned. Does this mean you have to walk on eggshells or agree with her every opinion? No. But the next time you are discussing the rise of alcoholism in indigenous peoples and she stomps off muttering that she knew you didn't think she was smart, now you'll know why. She is a rowboat.

and fun, the emotional equivalent of touch football. A heated discussion about politics may be, from your point of view, a heated discussion about politics, but from your GF's point of view, it can quickly devolve into "Why are you looking at me that way?" to "Why are you yelling at me?" to "You don't love me anymore." It's discord to her and it's personal. The original subject of the discussion is quickly forgotten, and faster than you can say, "Honey, are you on crack?," you're fighting about your relationship. Unfortunately, we're silly that way.

## Gasoline on a Fire

Fights come in all shapes and sizes, but there are common stumbling blocks. Watch out for them so they don't trip you up. Here are the top ten reasons for couples' scuffles.

1. **Money.** Money makes people scared, and scared people become angry people very quickly.

2. **Time.** As in not enough spent on her.

3. **Stress.** We know it's obvious, but not only does it weaken your immune system and give you wrinkles, stress also makes us all fly off the handle for no reason.

4. **Not listening.** It really pisses us off. If you can't pay attention when she's talking, you better get really good at faking it.

5. **Taking her for granted.** She is so good to you, so easy to be with, that you get used to it. She slips into

your pocket with the loose change, gum wrappers, and old lint. What is required is attention to detail—her details, your attention.

**6. Teasing.** Don't make fun of your girlfriend in front of others. She will probably be a good sport but will pay you back in spades later.

**7. Window shopping.** You may think you're getting away with paying attention to other girls, but we guarantee it does not go unnoticed.

**8. Gifts.** We have provided a whole chapter on this issue of what we like to call the "present tense." Ignore at your own peril.

**9. Being late.** Yes, we know we're not always on time, and we know it's a double standard, but if you guys are even fifteen minutes late, we take it as a personal insult. There. We've admitted it. And we still aren't going to do anything about our own lateness.

**10. Forgetting:***

Her birthday.

That she takes Sweet'n Low in her coffee.

That she is allergic to kiwi fruit.

That she has class every Tuesday night ("Where are you going?").

That she hates Thai food.

That she has a mushroom phobia.

*(\* Not remembering = not caring)*

## *A Bear on a Bicycle*

A lot of fights occur because of a fundamental gap in the problem-solving techniques of men and women. Actually, it's not a gap—it's more like the Grand Canyon. Men always assume women want advice and solutions to problems, but we just want a sympathetic ear. Let's say your GF comes and tells you she's had a fight with her mother and it's keeping her awake at night. "Look," you tell her, "this always happens with your mother. You'll feel better if you skip ahead and apologize, and by the way, where do you want to go tonight—Italian or seafood?" She flares up or gets sullen, says she hates Italian, and seafood makes her sick. The ball is off and running. You are in a fight.

What happened?

You think you're being helpful and showing love by offering a solution, but your GF interprets this "Let's fix it" attitude as invalidating her feelings, and it pisses her off. Don't hand her an answer, even if it's a good one. She just wants you to listen. Don't tell her that her mother has a point, that it's a simple misunderstanding, and why doesn't she pick up the phone and call. Your girlfriend needs to give you a word-for-word replay about her argument, and she wants the space to vent, to describe her mother's body language, her hairstyle, and the horrible brooch she wore. Moreover, she wants to be able to tell you about the time when she was eight and her mother wouldn't spring for the Suzy Homemaker Oven, and isn't this really the same thing all over again.

We know a BF who thinks this request for empathy over advice is like asking a bear to ride a bicycle. His opinion? "If you bring me a problem, I'm going to need to fix it, because that's what guys do. If you want something solved, bring it over. If you want a sympathetic ear, take it to the girls' team." We know it's tough to believe something so counterintuitive could be the right response, but trust us about this. When your girlfriend is upset, don't go wading in with a life jacket to save her, even if you feel responsible for her problem. Swim around in the water with her, or keep her company from the shore. The life jacket and your list of ideas will be appreciated later, when she's stopped flailing about in deep water.

---

**Women want empathy, not advice, and certainly not a quick fix.**

**YOU SAY:**                          **SHE HEARS:**

*"Honey, the solution is .......* *"You're too hysterical*
*obvious"* *to be smart."*

*"No need to get upset".......* *"You're handling this badly."*

*"Why are you crying?" ........* *"You're silly to feel that way."*

*"Didn't you decide what .....* *"I don't want to hear*
*to do already?"* *about this again."*

Now, her hearing may be correct—you may not want to empathize; you may want to fix it and move on. Too bad; girls don't work that way.

## *Cry Me a River*

You fight with your girlfriend, and she ends up crying, and you don't like it. She doesn't like it, either. However, tears are not the manipulative ploy that many men make them out to be. Sure, a handful of women believe that if at first you don't succeed, cry, cry, again. But believe us when we say that most women don't like to cry. For one thing, it ruins our makeup faster than you can say "color-correct moisture foundation with added sunscreen." For another, it's hard to be coherent through our snufflings.

Though guys hate the sound, sight, and proximity to tears, crying can be a good thing, because it's one of the ways your GF gets through the process of fighting. It's a package deal that comes with having a vagina. It's what she does. So don't freak out, and don't get mad. She's not going to break. We know that when your girlfriend cries, you get the guilts: "Oh God, I'm a jerk, I'm a bully." It's a reaction that seems to be hardwired into you guys from when you were little tykes. Boys are not supposed to hurt little girls or make them cry (you got in big trouble for sending Gail Griener blubbering to her teacher in the fourth grade), and a part of you is stuck on that playground.

We get it. It's hard to watch your GF cry. Who wouldn't feel bad? When she cries, you feel you must apologize, even if you're the injured party, which seems pretty unfair. Here is the good part: You can comfort your crying GF without feeling guilty, without apologizing, and without giving up your point of view. Let her cry. She needs to do it; it's the way she's made. You couldn't separate John McEnroe's volatile outbursts from his game. It was an integral part of how he played. And crying is a fundamental part of how your girlfriend communicates.

## Anger Management

It's hard to go further into this chapter without sounding like a self-help book (make sure you're being heard; never start a sentence with "you always"; anger is a sign that boundaries have been crossed; men are from Mars, women are from Bloomingdale's, etc.). If you want to go in-depth on the subject, buy another book, because fighting is really important, and it's really important to fight well. But here are a few practical guidelines:

- **Talk!** Silence is for prisoners of war. In your GF's mind, your silence means you don't care.

- **Fight to the finish.** Taking your marbles and walking away is for first-graders.

- **Listen.** You have to listen to what she's saying, whether or not you agree. That bears repeating—*whether or not you agree.*

- **Stick to what's true for you.** Tell her the truth from your point of view, and KISS (keep it simple, stupid), i.e., "It sucks what you did, and I'm really pissed off."

- **Fair fighting only.** This is no less true now than it was in preschool. No calling names, hitting, biting, or pulling hair.

- **Stay even so you don't have to get even.** Don't silently keep score or make a list of grievances that you carry around in your head. You'll only blow up later over the smallest thing, which will make you look like a psycho-rageaholic.

## Women Behaving Badly

Often you boyfriends don't hold your girlfriends to the same standards you would a man. You ascribe her bad behavior to "That's what women are like," when really it's bad behavior. If a guy acted that way, you would rip him a new one or take him out behind the proverbial woodshed. When it's your GF, you sweep it under the rug of "All women are crazy." We understand the impulse: If you are in Japan and someone doesn't shake your proffered hand, you don't take it as an insult. If you are in France and the waiter is rude, you take it in stride. If you are a guest in an igloo and find your nose being rubbed, you don't consider it forward. And because your GF is beyond the city limits of your understanding, you cut her a lot of slack. Let us give you some advice: Don't! Don't put up with a lot of bad behavior simply because she's a girl. It's not good for you and ultimately, it's not good for her. (How do you think Naomi Campbell got started?) Stick up for yourself. Worst-case scenario, you can always leave. Your GF doesn't have to hang around when you treat her badly, and vice versa.

## *Anything You Say May Be Used Against You*

Here's another one of those baffling contradictions. Because your GF will interpret a heated discussion as a fight, and because she cries a lot, it would follow that she might be at a disadvantage when you argue. Here's the thing: She's not. Once your GF puts the key in the ignition and it comes down to an actual fight between the two of you—especially *about* the two of you—she can outmaneuver you the way a Maserati can outmaneuver a Prius.

Your GF can talk rings around you, and she has a memory like a pawnbroker for grievances. She'll say, "That's not what you said two weeks ago," and she'll be right. Word for word. She has spent a lifetime mapping out relationships and memorizing the treasure maps to find the hidden meaning. When an argument occurs, she knows the territory: facts, feelings, old conversations, gestures, and facial tics. She knows all the significant landmarks, what they mean, and how to use them.

> *Your girlfriend has left a trail of bread crumbs in order to find her way home to her justified position, whereas you gobbled them up, thinking you'd never have to travel that way again.*

You guys can find Shea Stadium faster than we can, but you can't find your way to the heart of the matter. You're programmed to read literal maps, not emotional ones. The only recourse a BF has is the equivalent of soldier's code: name, rank, and serial number. It sounds like this: "Whatever I said, I didn't mean, and whatever I didn't say, I wish I had." Sure, you would prefer it if anything you said six months ago were inadmissible in an argument. You'd like for any and all comments to become null and void after seven days. Which would explain why men have aspired to be the Strong Silent Type. Unfortunately, that only works on film. In real life, women will take the strong and obliterate the silent.

## Fight Club

In the same way that it's important to know which cards are wild when you are playing Crazy Eights, it helps to distinguish what kind of fight you are in. You wouldn't play soccer with a mask and flippers, and you wouldn't show up to the opera in your swimsuit. You need to be prepared. Here are some classics:

**Frequent Fighter Program.** You fight so often, you could fly round-trip to Bali with all those bonus miles you've earned. Since this is one club in which you don't want elite status, we suggest changing airlines.

***National Association of Daddy's Girls.*** You're an unwitting member of this club if you're dating a girl who was loved too much or not enough by Daddy. You can't measure up, and you can't fix the damage, so check the membership directory for the name of a good therapist—for both of you.

***WAM Alliance.*** You can be a member of this group without knowing that "WAM" stands for "What About Me?" If this seems to be your GF's motto, pay your dues on time—that means paying your GF the love and attention she craves—and you won't have to attend the weekly meetings.

***Hypochondriac Association.*** You've signed up for a club that believes the relationship's immune system is compromised and needs constant monitoring. The credo is "How are we?" or "Are you okay?" If you find yourself a member of this club, our best advice is to get her a hamster she can mother.

***The Loyal Order of Sissies.*** Doesn't matter what your lodge number is, sissies cry when their knees get skinned by a good debate. The meeting is always called to order with a discussion of current events or the weather and always concludes with how you don't love her enough. If you find yourself in this club, throw her back in the water until she grows up.

***Phi Beta Look at Me!*** You pledged this fraternity when you started dating a GF who flirted with every guy she met. Her insatiable need for attention should be addressed ASAP, but don't get your hopes up that she will change. If she needs to be loved by all, she's never going to be satisfied loving just one, even if you are the greatest thing since sliced bread.

***"But I Thought We Were Just Talking" Society.*** Have you ever been in the middle of a nice conversation with your GF when all of a sudden you find yourself thrown on the floor with your windpipe crushed under her rage? Sorry to say, but you've been initiated into the "But I Thought We Were Just Talking" Society (also known as the "Blindside Club"). This club is called to order when you accidentally say something stupid or step on a sore spot of hers. Your GF has been triggered. So apologize for upsetting her and let the steam die down before you sort it out.

## Who's Sorry Now?

The 1970 movie *Love Story* brought us the enduring phrase "Love means never having to say you're sorry." Sorry (!), but that's such a piece of saccharine drivel that we suspect Ali MacGraw's character died from diabetes, not cancer. On the other end of the spectrum, a Shakespearian BF whose sweet words and jaunty codpiece wooed his GF into the woods more than once was right on the money when he said, "The course of true love never did run smooth."

Misunderstandings, mistakes, and mix-ups are a daily occurrence in the life of a love affair, we know that. We also know that asking a man to say "I'm sorry" is like asking a pig to fly. You may think you're saying "I'm sorry," but it comes out something like this:

- Oh, come on, I did not.

- I thought it would bring us closer together.

- I told you I shouldn't be around your mother.

- What do you want from me?

- But you said not to tell you.

- You're blowing this out of proportion!

- Honey, it didn't mean a thing.

- Eh?

Here's our list of ways to say you're sorry that will satisfy your GF and let you both move on. And you can do it without actually pronouncing those two little words you seem to think will make you spontaneously combust, break out in a rash, or instantly grow breasts. They will smooth things without your having to cop to anything.

- I wish I hadn't done that.

- I was feeling scared.

- I never meant for that to happen.

- Can you ever forgive me?

- I wish I could do it all over again.

- You know I love you so much.

- I'm in the doghouse, aren't I?

- Can we do instant replay?

- Let me try that again.

- Should I make a bed on the couch now or later?

- Well, I think that deserves a spanking.

## BE PREPARED

Your GF will discuss every fight with her girl posse. Everything will be analyzed to death before being resurrected and analyzed again. Days, weeks, and months after the fight is over, your girlfriend's girlfriends will remember what happened and bring it up to her when a new fight arises. In a way, you're not having a fight with one woman, you're having a fight with a harem. If only this rule applied to sex.

## *A Fighting Chance*

The last thing you guys want to do is come home and be faced with power struggles and combat skirmishes. You get enough of that out in the big bad world. But when a GF is feeling lonely, abandoned, or plain old neglected, she'll resort to fighting just to get a dial tone. We know it's exactly what our boyfriends hate, but what's a girl to do? When men are preoccupied—whether it be with work or money or the season finale of *The Sopranos*—women interpret it as rejection. If you find yourself in this position, consider that she might be starved for attention before trading her in for a new model. Sometimes picking a fight is really about missing you.

# CHAPTER 19

# BUT I THOUGHT IT WAS GOING SO WELL

**A lot of things seem like a good idea at the time.** That explains disco, hair scrunchies, the mullet, and the Vietnam War. It also explains some relationships (think David Spade and Heather Locklear). Even with the best of intentions and the best-laid plans, a seemingly happy relationship can quickly go south. One moment everything is smooth sailing, the sea is calm, the sky is blue, and love is in the air. Then, faster than you can say "But I thought it was going so well," your calm seas turn choppy and the same powerful forces that drove you together now propel love's fragile schooner toward perilous rocky shoals.

Batten down the hatches, my friend—you have just entered the Bermuda Triangle of relationships: jealousy, cheating, and breaking up.

### Green-Eyed Monster

Boy meets girl. Boy gets girl. Boy stalks girl in an attempt to confirm his suspicion that girl is sleeping with his college roommate.

When we see someone getting what we want or what we believe is ours, jealousy rears its ugly head. An equal-opportunity aggressor, jealousy is the chicken pox of emotions:

> **Your jealous feelings are exhausting, addictive, and a complete waste of time. But you have to attend to them. Think of it like an appointment at the proctologist's. Your instinct may be to ignore them and hope they will go away, but you'll be much better off if you get in, fix the problem, and get out. You don't want to spend all day there. It's not Circuit City.**

Few people escape this itchy, uncomfortable, and unhappy experience. It afflicts everyone. And it brings out the worst in everyone. GFs become clingy, insane, and obsessive. BFs become belligerent, paranoid, and mean. When you're a teenager, it can feel kind of cool to be crazy jealous of your GF. It's dramatic; romantic, even. Your young GF gets to be a vulnerable treasure in danger of being stolen, while you get to try on the role of tough guy protecting what's yours. That may be fine when you're sixteen, but behave that way as an adult, and you're likely to end up on Court TV.

When jealousy comes up between you and your girlfriend—and chances are it will—it can be nearly impossible to tell who's to blame and how to fix it. Let's take a sample situation, look at it from different perspectives, and figure out where the problem lies.

### The Situation:

Your ex is in town and asks you to have coffee. You decide to go, and your GF gets jealous.

*IS IT:*
*A) a misunderstanding?*
*B) her?*
*C) you?*

*A)* If it's a misunderstanding it's an easy call. Your GF remembers how you've talked about this old flame, and thinks your reminiscing is actually residual love. Understandably, she gets jealous. If you kindly and sincerely let her know the nature of your true feelings, and reassure her that she has nothing to worry about, she will look in your eyes, see your sincerity, and calm down.

*B)* What if the problem is with her? Your girlfriend knows there is nothing between you and your ex, but hell will freeze over before she'll let you out of her sight with another woman. Even your Aunt Edna is a problem for her. It's not because you're not trustworthy, it's because she's paranoid and would like a restraining order that prevents you from getting within a hundred yards of another woman. If you happen to be with a girl like this, we hope you don't mind being kept on a short leash.

*C)* What about the unlikely event that these jealous feelings are being caused by you? Okay, be honest, there's still some sexual chemistry between you and your ex that your GF rightly picks up on. She remembers the way you've talked about your ex and wonders why you are recklessly putting yourself in temptation's way. Is it possible that you and your new GF are getting too intimate for your comfort level? If so, then we can understand why coffee with your ex sounds like such a good idea—in the same way throwing matches in a roomful of gasoline sounds like a good idea. Just don't be surprised when your new relationship goes KABOOM! and you're blown right into single waters, because that was your intent all along.

## Are You the Jealous Type?

If you find yourself in the middle of a jealous tirade, camped out in front of her house spying because you've convinced yourself she isn't out with the girls at all, take a breath and apply some Boy Scout principles. Don't try to make your way out of the wilderness when the visibility is poor and you don't have the compass of your rationality. Sit down and ask yourself the following questions. Have you ever been accused of being:

- overly possessive?

- someone who never trusts his GF?

- chronically insecure?

If you answered yes to any of these questions, then you probably have jealous tendencies. That's a big load to carry and will only generate unhappiness in you and those around you. In the long run it will give you wrinkles and thin lips. Don't underestimate the power of jealousy to sabotage your life. It's a man eater, and no one can get that monkey off your back but you. So get some help with it: therapy, prayer, good old-fashioned soul-searching, or whatever you do to exorcise your personal demons. Of course, it could be that you're just a straight-ahead asshole, in which case there's no help for that. But we doubt it. You wouldn't be reading this book if you were.

Let's take it one step further. Sometimes your GF is giving you just cause for jealousy. Maybe she's feeling unappreciated and is trying to get your attention. She could be trying to tell you something (albeit in a fucked-up way). She could be trying to spur you into action. Our friend Jessica came home one day and told her BF that Sylvester Stallone had hit

## BE PREPARED

### THE RIDDLE OF THE SPHINX

There are men and women out there who want only what they can't have. We've all seen them or (shudder) have even been one. She complains about how there are no nice guys out there while stepping over their carcasses to get to another womanizing jerk. What you have to understand is that she's telling you what she wishes she wanted, not what she actually wants. To be with this woman (chances are she'll be super-hot and great in bed), you have to suppress your sweeter impulses and act like a dick to keep her interested. And pretty soon you're not acting anymore.

on her in the parking lot of the Universal CityWalk. "Yeah," she said, "he stepped out of his stretch limo and invited me to lunch." Naturally, it was all made up, and why she chose Sly (wouldn't Johnny Depp have been just as easy?) is clearly a testament to her desperation, but you see the lengths we can be driven to by neglect. Acting this way may be manipulative and immature. It may piss you off. But address it with patience; she may have a point.

## High Fidelity

It was Henry Kissinger who said, "Just because you're paranoid doesn't mean they're not out to get you." It was Mae West who said, "A hard man is good to find," and it was Sigmund Freud who said, "Sometimes a cigar is just a cigar." To that we say, "Unless that cigar is being smoked by a hard man in his boxers, and then you really have a reason to be paranoid."

Everybody has different theories as to what constitutes cheating. Naughty e-mails? Kissing at parties? Everybody draws the line in a different place. Where do you stand on the politics of cheating? Some men were inspired by the Clinton era and don't consider a blow job "sexual relations with that woman." Others, whose roots can be traced back to the Carter administration, are racked with guilt over having sinned in their hearts.

The question remains: How do you define cheating? Is there a scale?

We're glad you asked. We've designed a fidelity device that measures the energy released by cheating in much the same way that the Richter scale measures the seismic energy released by an earthquake. Consider this:

**Less than 3.5.** Generally not felt, but recorded by you. This includes activities that can be enjoyed without any dangerous side effects, such as flirting with the girl at the Piggly Wiggly.

**3.5–5.4.** Often felt, but rarely causes damage. Your GF will note that you're flirting with the waitress or the gas meter girl, but she thinks it's cute and nonthreatening.

**Under 6.0.** Slight damage to well-designed relationships, but can cause major damage to poorly constructed GFs whose infrastructure is weak. Most GFs file "Under 6.0" as boys-will-be-boys activities, such as being chatted up at parties or adored by random females.

**7.0–7.9.** Major earthquake. Can cause serious damage over larger areas of relationship. You are teetering on the edge, and your GF is right to be worried about how sturdy you are. 7.0–7.9 can include The Tongue and is in danger of leading to extracurricular nookie.

**8 or greater.** Relationship quake. We don't want to be crude, but putting it in is putting it in, and no spin doctor can dress up that one. If your flirting has progressed to unadulterated adultery, it will cause serious damage in areas several hundred kilometers across your relationship. Watch out for falling debris.

Flirting with someone you find attractive, whether it be over the Internet, over the Xerox machine, or across a crowded room, is addictive, and it's hard to do just once. Sexy e-mails will satisfy you until they don't satisfy you anymore, and then you'll have to step it up. Kissing at a party makes you want to kiss more. That's the thing about flirting—you either have to knock it off or step it up. The sexual arousal dance is like a drug and actually stimulates the dopamine in your brain. It kicks in your hormones and kicks out your common sense. You may know it's harmless flirting, but your body doesn't. It thinks it's the real deal, and pretty soon your body will start to convince your mind. Our advice is to keep yourself out of temptation's way. Don't put yourself in the position where you have to depend on your big head to overrule your little head. That will never happen.

---

We have always marveled at how men and women talk about infidelity. "It just happened," they say, as if there they were, innocently walking along, minding their own business, when wham! They tripped and landed with their genitalia tangled up in someone else's.

## *Your Cheating Heart*

First, there are the obvious reasons for cheating, shared by both sexes:

- We are not into you anymore.

- We know you're not into us anymore.

- We've met someone who—in that moment—seems to be the answer.

- We are revenge cheating to get back at you so we don't feel powerless anymore.

- We need to get out of what we are in and into something new.

- We always wanted to sleep with another girl. (Okay, this is just a GF thing.)

And then there is the reason that belongs solely to you guys. You know that voice in your head that says, "But I have to fuck her, because someday I will be dead, and I won't have fucked her." Women don't really have a companion voice to this, so we don't understand the power of the primal impulse "must fertilize ALL of them"; but we know that it pulls you around like a water-skier holding on to the *Queen Mary*.

## *Red-Handed*

It doesn't take CSI to uncover your cheating. Chances are, it will be revealed through the small—stupid!—things you do: your cell phone log, the phone bill, the e-mail you forgot to erase, the pair of panties in your back pocket, the neighbor who saw you together, whatever. Although we're not fans of cheating, we would be remiss in our duties as purveyors of practical tips if we didn't give you insight into the two ploys your girlfriend will use to make you spill the beans. And you fall for them every time.

### *She'll say:*

"It's okay, I'm not mad—you can tell me. I just want the truth."

— OR —

"I already saw you together, read the note, spoke to Susie, whatever [fill in the blank]—so don't bother to lie."

### *You'll respond with:*

"Okay, as long as you want the truth and aren't mad."

— OR —

"How did you find out?"

Either way, the jig is up.

At least you can't say we didn't warn you.

> Our friend Paul called his GF by the wrong name. He passed it off as a blunder, a simple mind fart, and they laughed about it. But during sex, he yelled out the wrong name again and found himself locked outside in the middle of the night in his skivvies. Cheating always, always, always comes out. We could counsel you to be more cautious, to be "ninja cheating guy," and while that might be good advice, it really just delays the inevitable. In a perfect world, cheating wouldn't exist, and "half the fat, all the taste" wouldn't be a lie, either.

You can be aware of these traps. And you should beware of them. Still, at a certain point, you've got to admit that trying to keep the details of your story straight (did you tell your GF the same thing last week that you told her last night?) is beyond your capabilities. As we said before, with few exceptions, people want to get caught. Why? Because carrying a secret around is at first thrilling, and then it becomes a burden. A secret becomes quite costly, and no one can operate under the strain of lying for long, except a sociopath.

### Common Courtesy

It seems odd to apply the idea of common courtesy to cheating, especially since, while it may be common, there's nothing courteous about it. Here's the thing. Your GF would rather be told about your cheating by you, not by the neighbor, phone bill, or talk-radio program. It is better to be a betrayed GF than a crazed female Sherlock Holmes scrambling for clues her BF may have left. Not being able to stop searching for something that will break your heart when you find it is an awful position to be in.

And yet, in all fairness, we have to cop to the fact that although we ask you to tell us, we can't guarantee we will take it well. Our pal Ben, who didn't have an exclusive with his GF, made a deal with her that they would tell each other if there had been any extracurricular sex (for health reasons). He dutifully told her and spent the next several weeks being blasted by her. He won't be sharing his adventures with her again anytime soon. And that's the rub. Our request to be told probably makes you guys think we're giving you a get-out-of-jail-free card. We're not. Still, you need to know that there are aspects of cheating that your GF will consider lower than low:

- Having sex in the same bed where you and your GF sleep. You're betraying your GF's trust. Do you have to be icky, too?

- Buying the other woman presents, then leaving them around for your GF to find.

- Keeping intimate items the other woman gave you: letters, bobby pins, clips, notes, underwear.

- Writing about it. Your notebook is a GF magnet. She will be inescapably drawn to read the damn thing.

- Parading the other woman around your circle of friends. You put everyone in an untenable position.

- Going to her favorite restaurant with the other woman.

- Having sex with her best friend or her sister. We know attraction is 80 percent proximity, but there must be other girls you are close to—some damage is irreparable.

## Signs That Your GF May Be Cheating on You

### Turnabout Is Fair Play

- She's cranky and dissatisfied (more than usual).

- She finds fault with everything, as if she's justifying her cheating by finding things wrong with the relationship and you.

- She's distant.

- When she leaves the house, she's looking particularly hot.

- She buys new underwear and doesn't model it for you.

- She starts losing weight. This could be for the other guy's benefit, or it could be due to the stress of lying to you.

- She doesn't want to take responsibility for any of the problems between you.

- You can't reach her; suddenly, she has inexplicable cell phone problems.

- She has new friends whom she doesn't want you to meet.

- You come home to find her in the shower with another guy.

- She invites you to her wedding—as an usher.

There are plenty of reasons not to cheat: You'll get caught; it will wreck your relationship; and lying, like cigarettes, is bad for you (it may not blacken your lungs but it blackens your soul). But when you're debating whether to stray or not to stray, your logical, rational voice has the mute button pushed. When you have cute Mary McCann up against the wall with her skirt hiked up, the inner debate on whether or not to go for it will be a short one.

You have to make the decision long before Mary McCann is whispering in your ear. If cheating seems like a viable choice to you, chances are you aren't ready to hang up your Player spikes just yet.

## Should I Stay or Should I Go?

A bad breakup can smash you into more pieces than Humpty Dumpty, and even all the king's horses and all the king's men won't be able to put you together again.

Here's the thing about breaking up: Typically, you have to do it three times to make it stick. The first time is too upsetting and your resolve is weak. The second time, the breakup/makeup sex is so good, it will convince you that you can still make it work. By the third time, you are willing to endure the drama and heartache required to put it all behind you and move on.

# BE PREPARED

Unfortunately, being cheated on usually makes it difficult to leave the relationship. Having your legs kicked out from under you can make it very tough to walk out the door. You may feel compelled to rush to a decision just to get away from the pain. Don't. Don't hire a moving van. Don't get engaged. And don't break up that minute. It's natural to want to have sex right away, to get close, to prove they still want you. Don't do that, either. Take a breath and sit with the pain. The answer will come. Observe more. Do less. For additional advice, watch reruns of *Melrose Place* or, for you younger studs, *The OC.*

A long, drawn-out breakup is agony, but some people need to squeeze every last drop of sweaty passion out of their dead love affair. A little bit of that may be fine for your *Casablanca* file of memories, but eventually you'll need to get it out of your system and let the poor beast die. Because we have seen the following scenario more than once: You keep playing this bizarre emotional back-and-forth game, when all at once she takes the initiative and ends it . . . and bam! You are back to square one, an emotional mess once again. Paul Simon came up with fifty ways to leave your lover, and we are sure that with the right bottle of tequila, we could make it one hundred. Just take a moment to review this brief list of *do's and don'ts* so that you're prepared when it's your turn to hit the road, Jack:

***Don't do a telemarketer.*** Breaking up over the phone is tacky and cowardly. Period.

***Don't pull a Ronald Reagan on her.*** You tell her girlfriends and hope the information trickles down.

***Don't let her down easy.*** We don't believe in this theory. You've made the decision, you've already broken up with her in your mind, but you haven't really told her. Not completely. Not straight out. Not in so many words. You're pretty sure she's got the idea, but you're taking it slow and starting ever so casually to date other girls.

***Don't Tarzan-date.*** Best to let go of one vine before you grab hold of the next one, otherwise you end up wounding your old girlfriend and letting your new one know you can't be trusted.

***Don't sad-song her.*** This is where you sing "Poor, Poor Pitiful Me" while doing all sorts of shitty things to make *her* leave you.

***Don't pull an Invisible Man.*** Don't disappear, avoid her phone calls, and hope you never see her again. You may justify your behavior because you are a jerk and bad for her anyway, but we GFs need to hear good-bye even from jerks.

We know that if you are planning on breaking up with her, doing it the right way might not be a priority. After all, what's in it for you? Sure, you don't want to hurt her, but making your soon-to-be-ex happy is no longer at the top of your agenda. We know it's easier to move to a different town and change your phone number. But don't. Here's why:

***Karma.*** What goes around comes around. Someday, God forbid, it will be you, and you will want her to give it to you straight.

***Reputation.*** There will inevitably be some tangential connection between your new girlfriend and the one you didn't break up with the right way. It is more dangerous to your reputation to break up badly than to just break up. It will get around—how do you think "all men are jerks" was started?

## What If She Breaks Up with You?

If she breaks up with you, there are survival techniques to get through the rough parts. First thing is to find some friends who confirm that she is a crazy nut job and that you are well rid of her. Repeat to yourself that she was never that great anyway.

Next step is to avoid the two extremes, the Jumper and the Hanger-on. The Jumper is the guy who starts to date immediately. The distraction can be helpful (and the sex can be great), but the side effects outweigh the good. You become like a contestant on *Survivor* who, having lost twenty-five pounds, takes up residence in a Cinnabon shop. You'll eat happily for six months straight, but you won't be in very good shape at the end of it. Don't play the game on the rebound. Go back to the starting line before you put yourself in the race again.

The Hanger-on, on the other hand, can't get over the breakup. We have all seen this person and most of us have even been this person. Months go by and there you are, still mourning a lost love, still boring your pals with wistful stories of Mandy. If you're stuck like this, the most useful advice we can give you here comes from our grandmothers: "Sometimes, the best way to get over someone is to get under someone."

## *Better Luck Next Time*

Everyone messes up in relationships. It's inevitable. The real test is how quickly you are able to clean it up. Does the mess lie around for days, attracting flies, or are you able to contain the spill and decontaminate the area within a relatively short period of time? More important, are you able to distinguish between the little "Hand me a paper towel" type of spill and the big "Let's rent a wet vac with a high-pressure extractor" kind of mess? And perhaps most important of all, are you able to recognize an extinction-level event, the kind from which no relationship can recover?

Traveling through the Bermuda Triangle of heartbreak is a rite of passage, and most people can't avoid it. For some, the hard lessons learned force the traveler to have greater appreciation for the good, since he is now intimately acquainted with the bad. Others don't get this benefit. They get lost in the Bermuda Triangle of pain and paranoia and never find their way out.

Your GF knows that finding a BF who has been through the troubled waters of love and come out the other side in one piece is a good thing. She knows a little history in suffering for love makes everyone more patient, willing, and loving the next time around. So if you manage to weather the storm of jealousy, cheating, and breaking up, you will be the kind of seasoned sailor we'll want on our boat. Remember: Every relationship is supposed to end, except the last one.

# CONCLUSION

*And that's all she wrote. We've given you the skinny, the* scoop, the straight dope, the what's good, and quite possibly the lowdown. We hope you regard this book not as a list of chores, complaints, and ways you must change, but rather as one that offers insights, translations, and inspiration. We do not encourage the cramming of this material. Take our recipes for success and make them your own: Add a few ingredients, leave a few things out, that way, when you dish it up, the meal is all you, and all she wants.

And speaking of all she wants, sometimes women make the mistake of insisting that the most important quality in a BF is that he understand his GF's needs and her emotional landscape. But it's not and you won't. More important than understanding her is accepting that her customs and concerns, like those of some foreign country, are integral to who she is, and that you must respect them even if they seem insane to you. (In some countries they think it's okay to eat dogs.)

So off you go, equipped with a good map and a reliable compass. We also suggest you pack a clean pair of underwear and a sense of humor.

Go get 'em, tiger.